170 Bible Poems

from the Heart
that Touch the Soul

BY: PAUL REVENSON

ISBN: 978-1-966954-09-5 (paperback)
ISBN: 978-1-966954-10-1(hardcover)
ISBN: 978-1-966954-11-8(ebook)

Library of Congress Control Number: 2025905557

170 Poems from the Heart that Touch the Soul

Bible Poems by Paul J. Revenson. . . Phil.1:6

  A truly readable, straightforward, warming, meaningful collection of original, Scriptually based poetry of which notable ministers and national theologians have favorably commented. If you chance to read this book, hopefully you'll be blessed to experience this timeless collection of inspired truth that not only a Bible lover, but openminded, lovers of classical literature might find interesting and enjoy-- that might touch the heart. . .reach and inspire the soul!

* If ye then be risen with Christ, seek those things which are above. Col.3:1

*Sing forth the honors of His Name, make His praise glorious. Psa.66:2

* I will make Thy Name to be remembered in all generations, therefore shall all the people praise Thee for ever and ever. Psa.45:17

* O how I love Thy Law. It is my meditation day and night. Psa.119:97

*Whatsoever things are true, whatsoever things are honest, whatsoever things are just, pure, lovely, and of good report. . .think on these things. Phil.4:8

"Paul Revenson loves to share the Gospel in music and poetry, and he does it with passion and conviction. You will find spiritual comfort and encouragement here."
—Dr. David Epstein, Senior Pastor,
 Calvary Baptist Church, N.Y.C. .

"Paul Revenson's poems are Biblically based and quite imaginative. They brim with truth and common sense, plus interesting rhymes. They are a great devotional source."
 —Frank Boggs, First vocal recording artist, Word Records/ Billy Graham-Charles Stanley, Atlanta, Ga.

"The poet has the uncanny talent to express the Christian worldview in both classical and contemporary flair. Each poem will speak to your heart and mind, and give you a deeper understanding of what it means to be a 'child of God'."
 —Brenda Milliner—35 years-N.Y.C. urban missionary.

"Your book,'160 Poems from the Heart': is aptly named and clearly Biblical. They express notions that we Christians share but don't often put in words.
Your poems bring glory to God. Thank you for seeing that I got a copy."
----Dr. R.C. Sproul
Author of 80 Christian books. Founder of Ligonier Ministries.

"Thank you, Paul, for sharing your craft, filled with powerful verse; a fine collection that stirs the heart, strengthens faith and provokes the soul!
I would like to recite some of your poems on my daily radio program? I'll be sure to mention the book's name and yours. People just need to read this meaty prose. . . It'll bless their hearts."
---Joni Eareckson Tada, Founder, CEO of Joni & Friends Int'l disability Center,
 Artist, author, speaker on WMCA radio.

Oh, How I Love Thy Word

How I love Thy Word, O God,
Its truth is my delight.
It helps to guide my path on earth,
It tells me wrong from right.

It nourishes my hungry heart,
it refreshes my dry soul.
It undergirds my stumbling steps,
it brings forth God's control.

O, how I love Thy precious Word,
when my heart is laden down—
its Psalms, the Proverbs, the Gospel books;
God's wisdom can be found!

But most of all, it speaks of Jesus—
God's sole Salvation plan—
of how He suffered for our sins,
and gave His life for man.

It's like a mirror that peers within,
to bring us near to God.
It's like a compass for a sailor,
it's like a shepherd's rod.

It tells us how to get to Heaven,
to avoid sin's perils vast.
I love Thy Word—forever blest,
and shall forever last.

Matt.4:4, Psa.119:97–105

The Answer to Life

When I see The Heavens—
 the work of God's Hands,
I ask: What is God's purpose here?
His creation. . .His desire to share?

Why did He, in His image, make man;
Was it love that dawned this "wond'rous plan"?
body, mind and soul...
so might he thrive and multiply;
would progress be his goal?
Inventing, building, enjoying life--
to aspire, labor, then to die. . .
to seek, study, and explore—
only to question why?

Why was man put on the earth...
his longing, his reward...
to test his loyalty to his God,
and to glorify the Lord.

Micah 6:8 What doth the Lord require of man but to
act justly, to love mercy and walk humbly before God.
Gen.1:1 In the beginning God created the Heavens and the Earth.
Isa. 45:18 He formed the earth to be inhabited.

Have You Been Born Again?

Have you been born again, my friend...
Have you embraced God's love?
Has Christ indwelt your heart and life,
which means...Born from Above?

Did you give heed that still small voice,
your thirsting heart its goal,
and did respond, the Spirit wooed,
and thus renewed your soul?

As Jesus said to Nicodemus:
Which still holds true as then—
The sole condition to enter Heaven:
"One must be Born Again!"
'Cause flesh and spirit at death do sever...
return their separate way.
How will you then stand with God,
when come that Judgment Day?

For flesh is flesh, and spirit, spirit—
and Heaven will depend—
not on our righteous deeds we've done,
but...were you Born Again?

That nightly discourse, recorded in John 3:3
between Nicodemus and Jesus, is probably
one of the most important doctrinal events
recorded in Scripture...next to John 14:6.

Happy is the Home

Happy is the home where God is there,
where He is honored by Scripture and prayer.
Blessed is the family where Christ has first place,
His Word is loved—before meals they 'say Grace'.

Happy is the parent—whose Godly advice
is lived out in love—so the child follows Christ!
The mother who teaches the love of the Savior,
the example she sets—molds her child's behavior.
Whose love for her husband, and
The love for his wife,
show forth such compassion,
which dispels ev'ry strife.
Blessed is the home where just before bed,
sweet prayers are said,
and the Scriptures are read.
Happy is the home—God's will they will seek,
and go to God's House...at least once a week.

Happy is the home, and truly is blest,
where Christ is a friend—
and an unseen Guest.

Joshua 24:15b

 Marriage and the home were first instituted by God before there was
ever any "man-made government"... and so when the home collapses,
 the whole nucleus of society falls with it...as one can sadly see
today.

A Mother

No other creature that God has made
could ever take the place---of a Mother. . .
who's the sweetest gift to bless the human race!

A source of life, a fount of love—
Of kindness, virtue, trust,
Who looks to Heaven for her strength,
Her faith in God...a must!

She calms the hurt, then cleans the dirt,
She alone...does it best!
She's there to care...to console, to hear,
For "service" is her quest!
And yet she suffers, sacrifices,
toils without pay.
Without her soothing smile of sunshine,
there'd be no Sunny Day!

Oh, who could take a mother's place,
Or yet surpass her love?
For all the qualities she has,
were given by God above.

Prov.31:28

The hand that rocks the cradle rules the World!

The Eagle

The God Whose Word, made ev'ry bird,
speaks quite well of the eagle.
Who proudly flies the endless skies,
with matchless style so regal.
With lofty stance and piercing glance,
No creature's view is keener.
Which stands so bold—in heat or cold,
with fearless, firm demeanor.
Then wisely gages its descent,
Begins its earthward flow.
And boldly soars with searching gaze—
then scans the earth below.
Empow'red with special grace and strength,
all elements he braves.
God made this creature so to fly
Above the clouds and waves!

Thus, likewise rise with Eagle's wings,
So might God's grace endue.
For He Who made the Eagle fly,
shall so thy strength renew.
For they that wait upon the Lord—
With faith, on Him rely,
Shall thus mount up with Eagle's wings,
And to the Heavens fly.

Isaiah 40:31
 The eagle is a symbol of grace, strength and freedom!
The same attributes we share through Christ.

The Only Way

Jesus is the only way
by which we must be saved;
from sin and Hell, and death as well,
whence once we were enslaved.
Jesus is the only way
to God—which we must come.
For Christ Himself said: "I am The Way!"
Besides Him, there is none!

Our true High Priest, Sovereign Lord,
Shepherd, Savior dear;
Who intercedes for all our needs,
and knows our ev'ry care.
And shows His precious wounds above,
before the Mercy Seat.
His stripes which heal,
His love so real,
His hands…His nail-pierced feet!

None other greater promise given,
No better covenant—
The Risen Christ…our "Glorious Hope",
His "Blood Signed" Testament'!
So shall we heed His Blessed Word,
And do what He did say,
And trust **alone** His Saving Grace,
For **Christ's** the only way!

John 14:6

A Door

A door is a way for going about.
It serves as a means to come in or go out.
As an entrance or exit...whichever you desire.
A seclusion for safety,
An escape from a fire.
It protects from the storm,
It lets in your friends.
The infinite uses of a door never ends!
But just one leads to Heaven, and Life Evermore!
The threshold is faith—
And Christ is the Door.

John 10:9

He Paid It All

I could feel the nails thrust through His veins,
the crimson drops...to cleanse all my stains.
My Savior strung, His flesh hung and torn--
My ransomed soul, from death, reborn!

He died, the Son of God for me,
So might death's vile sting canceled be!
He did it all! Thus did my Savior bleed.
He paid it all! I have been freed.
Above all else, I know no need,
for Jesus paid it all.

Heb. 10:14

MY FAITH IS IN THE LORD

My heart is stayed on God.
His precepts I shall seek;
with faith and hope and grace--
His strength,
sustains me when I'm weak!
My love springs forth from Him.
My heart to Him—submit:
My future plans, His blessing stands,
if I'll my way---commit!
My life rests in His hands.
My soul He will preserve—
and grant me courage to press on,
that I my Lord may serve.
My soul He has restored,
while Him I'll follow yet,
for all I have I'll give to Him,
which choice I'll ne'er regret.

My loyalty shall be,
to Him Who died for me,
and dwell with Him in that Fair Land--
for all Eternity!

Psa. 17:15

Saving faith cannot be in religion, human ideology,
or good works but only in 'the Person of Jesus Christ'!

Incomprehensible

What grace, no mortal tongue could tell.
What love, no mind can comprehend!
Christ gave His life, so full and free—
Beyond the love of any friend.
What sacrifice, Who bore the Cross!
What wondrous love shown on the Tree.
What infinite grace, that God Himself
would save a sinner. . .lost like me!

Yet further still—that God would care
for sinful man,
so fallen, wretched, hopeless, blind—
that on the Cross would take my place...
exceeds the thought of human mind!

Only in Glory might I behold—
my comprehension might begin:
That blood once shed long years ago,
might cleanse away the darkest sin.

Eph.2:7

"And sinners plunge beneath the flood,
  lose all their guilty stains." Old hymn

Said the Monkey to His Uncle

Asked the Monkey to his uncle:
"Is Mister Man our next of kin?"
"Why I hope not, naïve nephew...
came this thought of Old Darwin?"
Replied the nephew, kind of puzzled:
"Cause to me this seems a sham...
We've no history of any Hitler,
Jack the Ripper, Son of Sam!"

In the zoo, it's true they keep us,
for a profit, it would stem.
Yet when they spend time at 'Rykers',
we don't go to visit them!"

You don't say that Distant Darwin
once ate bananas and used our tail,
is now teaching this as "Science",
at Harvard, Princeton, even Yale?
But whose dilemma actually caused it,
was it our fault, was it his?
We're not the ones to face Hell-fire,
it's the 'unsaved man' who is!

Are they slandering us, dear Uncle,
by associating guilt,
because the thought of Evolution's
such an 'insult' to the hilt!"

Genesis 1:27

God gave "Moses" the Ten Commandments---
He didn't give them to "a monkey"!

God's Name Is Holy

To take God's Holy Name in vain…
Such person must be so insane!
Whose soul and mouth so vile, debased,
Whose spiritual life---'tis but a waste!
Who have no knowledge of Blessed God,
Whose sinful life is surely hard.
The way of Peace they have not known.
For thus they'll reap what they have sown!
For thus the Christ they do not know,
So straight to Hell they'll surely go.
Their cursing, damning will not quell,
Their tongues will take them—
Straight to Hell!
The Word of God speaks very plain—
"Thou shalt not take God's Name in vain"!
For God will take so much abuse,
'til they face Christ with no excuse!
Why not use Mohammed's, Buddha's,
or Krisna's name?
Because their names are "already" in vain!
But my dear Lord Jesus—for me Who came--
To bring Salvation through His Name!
And reign on High with Him—forever!
Degrade that Name?
God forbid it ever!
So repent—kneel at the cleansing fount,
For some day you will give account!
This message written very plain:
"Thou shalt not take God's Name in vain"!

Exod.20:7. Matt.12:36

Jesus said: "For everyone shall give an account
of every idle word that they have spoken!" Wow!

Ode to a Godless Poetry Recital

I see certain silhouettes, sulking sounds—
Reciting, not exciting. . .wisdom wanting.
Who can fathom what was said?
Much better lyrics I have read.
And what I heard. . .seemed strained and blurred.
How tragic—so void of sense and 'verbal magic'. . .
Of which I heard.

No word of truth, of grace,
of hope, to touch the soul;
Its very voidness takes its toll.

Still straining-- empty forms seem to lean,
to struggle
Deep within—
to draw out what they mean?
Uneasy, time-tortured...
Creative lore hard-pressed.
To call it "Poetry", as a poet—
I detest!

Let Sound and Fury take its toll—
Since God and truth have left the soul.

Ecclesiastes 1:14

How tedious and tasteless the hours. . .when Jesus no longer I see!

I Heard the Voice as an Angel

I heard the voice as an Angel sing
Upon my listening ear.
Its gentle sweetness felt so warm,
As it soared from a glistening sphere.

Its purest kindness brought such peace,
As through my mind it streamed.
It touched my soul, and did unfold
Much fairer than a dream.

My eyes beheld while joy had welled,
In deepest peace caressed.
Its power to heal and love now sealed
A hope that soothed and blessed.

I heard the voice as an Angel sing,
Though just that once befell.
O, when shall I ever hear it again?
No dream on earth could tell.

The Song I'd heard this 'Angel' sing,
Which fair yet rare occurred,
Was naught but the **Gospel** my Savior brought,
Whence I opened my heart to God's Word.

Psalm 119:103

No voice can sing nor heart can frame, nor can the memory find,
a sweeter sound than Thy blest Name, O Savior of mankind.

14

Cast Thy Care on Him

Cast thy burden on the Lord—
Thus shalt thou be sustained.
Whence murmuring and bickering,
mightst nothing e'er be gained.

God cares for you to see you through,
midst morning, night or noon,
to lift you toward the "mountain-top",
above life's valley's gloom.

He hears thy cry and follows by
to lift thy weary load,
for Christ Himself didst bear our sins—
whence climbing 'Calvary's Road'.

"I am the way"-- O, hear Him say,
"Come unto me and rest",
Thence cast thy burden on the Lord;
Might He restore thy zest!

Cast all thy care on Him in prayer,
For Christ doth care for you.
For they that trust and wait on Him,
Shall sure their strength renew.

1 Peter 5:7

Be careful for nothing, but prayerful about everything!
'Cast thy burden on the Lord and He shall sustain thee.'

So Let Us Run

We have been called to "Run the Race"…
Life's "endless battles" we must face!
And with each weight being laid aside,
we must in faith—God's Word confide;
And lawfully strive within God's rule,
though the World "might think that you're a fool"!
Though the Adversary--we may not see,
yet through the Cross of Calvary—
we must--by Grace, the battle win,
against the World, the flesh and sin!

For it's "How We FINISH"…**not** how we start,
So guard against doubt's fiery dart.
Ye must then keep God's armor on,
His grace and Spirit, rely upon.

Our flesh and self must be kept down,
if we would win a "Victor's Crown"!
It's not to the strong, nor to the swift,
nor he who bears a special gift',
But to the humble, faithful saint,
who keeps the faith, and does not faint!

So don't despair, still run the race,
'til we see Jesus face to face--
and know at last…the race is won!
When we hear those words:
"My child, well done"!

Heb.12:1

"Be not weary in well-doing,
for in due season ye shall reap
if ye faint not!"

I'll Trust Him 'Til The End

There's no true gain of victory--

Lest Jesus we confide;

Midst trials, storms and Hell's attacks...

Lest Jesus be beside!

When all seems sad, depressed and dark,

without a ray of hope;

yet still the Master stands nearby--

'til there's no more end of rope!

His trusting Hand and Word shall stand,

Despite what seems to be...

For He will never let me down,

for I know He cares for me!

With Him I'll fight the "Good Fight of Faith",

For life's battle's never done.

But only with my eyes on Christ,

'til the final battle's won.

2 Tim. 4:7

Communion

The table of the Lord was spread,
As Jesus reached and took the bread.
Then to His twelve disciples said:
"Unto a cross. . .I'll soon be led".

While there the twelve just sat and thought,
So clear the message there was brought,
How man's Salvation would be wrought,
How sin and death would soon be fought!

While Judas lurked within His sight,
Christ's face had shone with Heaven's light.
What deed had seemed a dreadful plight,
Would soon turn out to man's delight!

The debt for sin, its penalty,
This cup, my Blood 'tis shed for thee.
Thus might Eternal Life be free--
Hence shall I go to Calvary!"

Matt.26:26

Thank You Jesus for taking my place, bearing my sins-
    by DYING ON THE CROSS AND RISING FROM THE GRAVE! Amen.

'A Wonderful Savior is Jesus my Lord!'

Good Friday

They led Christ through Gethsemane,
Where prayed He all night long.
Came Judas paid. . . Hell's vile parade;
Most envious, hateful throng.
One of Christ's twelve, being paid, betrayed—
Approached to kiss his Lord. . .Such was the kiss
 that Judas brought. . .perdition, his reward!

 They seized the Savior, with hands of hate,
that sinless, healing Lamb.
Then cruelly wrenched Him from His friends,
who then did all disband.
Whence having left Him there to face—
unjustliest mocking trial,
Whom taunted, spat on, beard they'd plucked...
Inhumanly reviled!
They'd knelt in mockery, jeered in hate—
spat in rudest scorn.
They flogged His back, no spite had lacked...
Chastisement's peace He'd born.

The darkest hour sin ever knew...
whence nailed Christ to that Tree...
hence trod the winepress all alone...
God could not look to see!
The Heavens bowed, the sun withdrew,
While there on Christ was placed---
the sins of every mortal soul
e'er born of Adam's Race.
Said last: . . ."I thirst"!
Took Christ--the curse,
with blood and breath diminished.
Still love remained, when last exclaimed,
with joyous shout:. . ."It's Finished!"
It was that Cross, a blood stained Cross,
where Jesus took my pain.
And from the tomb, an Empty Tomb,
where Jesus rose again!
Gethsemane, to Calvary,
Redemption reached its goal!
From Heaven. . .why, to earth to die?
Because---He loved man's soul.

1 John 4:10, Rom.5:8
The greatest love ever shown. . . .at CALVARY!

When Jesus Bore the Cross

Jesus took the curse for me,
the day they nailed Him to a tree.
The price of all my sin was paid—
when He into a tomb was laid.
What penalty...He took my stead—
when Jesus to a cross was led.
What love was shown, what price was paid,
When in Gethsemane He prayed.
What anguish, pain, what agony—
when Jesus hung on Calvary.
What grace displayed, what mercy shown,
when He for me, my sins atoned!
What sorrow, death...what bitter loss—
when Jesus bore that heavy Cross.
What prize in Glory—what gift He gave,
when Jesus triumphed o'er the grave!
What wond'rous glory I shall see—
when Jesus shall return for me.

Heb.9: 28

Resurrection

Yes, we shall all be changed...
In "the twinkling of an eye"!
From dust to dust we go,
though the soul shall never die!
Unless a kernel falls...
is buried in the ground,
like manner, we shall rise—
when we hear that Trumpet sound!

What mystery shall be,
when we shall all be raised!
Eternal life—God's gift;
Might Jesus Christ be praised!

Christ first has gone before,
thus ne'er to die again,
then came back thus to prove,
that death is not the end!
The Word of God is true!
Philosophy—a fraud.
Absent from "this house",
means "Present with the Lord"!

Our loved ones we shall meet,
great things God has in store,
when we shall all be changed--
as Christ. . .forevermore!

1 Cor.15:51

We, as believers, have been given a great hope--
as an anchor to the soul!

Thanks Mom

There's no sense crying for you Mom,
You're not here anyhow.
You've met the Savior—seen His smile,
Yes, that's where you are now.
Done with pains, done with sorrows,
Where all sin is past.
And looking down the vale of time,
Oh, how life went fast.
All the years you spoke of Heaven,
Told others of that Land.
So now you're there with all your friends...
Oh Mom, it must be grand!
You met the Lord, you spoke to Jesus,
You actually saw His smile!
And now you're there with all the saints. . .
Tell 'em. . . I'll be a while.
And, Oh, to think you're now in Glory,
Your feet have trod on gold!
to be forever with the Lord—
Where never you'll grow old.
I'd like to see how you would smile,
As when your friends you meet.
But lest I make it there with you,
My joy won't be complete.
I thank you Mom, for teaching me
The Way to get to Heaven.
As with His love and songs I learned,
Before I reached age seven!
My lips were taught John 3:16,
My first words were your songs...
And now you're actually in that place
For which your heart had longed.
I'll thank you most for telling me
Of Heaven. . .where you did go.
And love you, 'til I see you Mom,
Where the greatest love we'll know.
  Your Son, Paul   Rev. 21:4

She Could Not Die

I stare and watch the tall trees wave,
while kneeling at my mother's grave;
And brush the sand...the grass not grown—
A rose, a ribbon . . .a lonely stone.
Dear mother, I know-- you did not die...
so why should I now stand and cry?
Your lovely face, like angel's bright—
now shut beneath the quiet night.
Your earthen form awaiting still,
now rests beneath the rolling hill.
Your sweetest hands, now fold in prayer,
the smile I loved, that gentle hair.
That face I loved, those bravest feet—
that preached the Gospel on the street!
Those gentle hands that gave out tracts,
and prayed for many on their backs.
Your spirit strong...forever free—
now soars above the waving trees.

I shall yet someday see you--ne'er need I pine,
for mother, you are doing fine.
'Cause where could be a better place—
but now in Heaven, near God's face.
And hear the voice of Christ so fair.
For surely Mother, you're not here!
Beneath this sod, you do not lie,
for mom, I know, you did not die!
You're now with Christ in fairest bliss,
no surer could I be of this.
As sure I leave this vacant place—
I know I'll see you face to face.
 As sure I stand beneath God's sky,
I know for sure. . . .you did not die.

To my mother, Leah...Paul.
John 11:25

We Have This Hope!

We shall see Him and be like Him,
O, what glorious, wondrous thought!
'Tis the hope we have in Jesus,
which the Word of God has taught.
Most mysterious truth unfolded,
reserved for those who but believe.
A gift given to God's children,
not like unto those who grieve.
O, what hope to know the Savior,
blest assurance, a place reserved.
'Tis the promise of the Savior—
who bear His Name, His Kingdom serve.
Thus changed we all shall be,
like unto Christ, Who ever lives.
For we shall see Him and be like Him,
and shall see Him as He is!

1Thes.4:13

We shall know Him by the nail prints in His Hands!

HEAVEN

What joy unspeakable-no soul hath dreamed,
That Land called Heaven, for those redeemed!
No ear hath heard, nor eye hath seen,
such place...God hath prepared!

What pure delight, none might describe,
blest "Book of Life"—whose names inscribed
from ev'ry nation, tongue and tribe—
be gathered 'round the Throne!

With walls of jasper,
Mid streets of gold...
With seraph chorus, bliss untold . . .
while countless ages still unfold. . .
ne'er mortal did behold!

Where tears are gone and pain is past,
and Satan into Hell is cast,
where perfect fellowship shall last forever,
and death has died!

None can imagine, nor words explain,
that Blessed Land, through Christ we'll gain,
and those who've suffered, in victory reign
with Him...forever and evermore!

For ne'er again shall there be night,
for Christ Himself shall be the Light,
and those by faith who "fought the fight",
shall hear His words..."Well done!"

No sin nor evil can abide,
where blood-bought saints are glorified,
for this---our Lord was crucified—
Mightst Heaven be our Home!

To dwell with Christ Eternally,
where all our loved ones we shall see,
O yes, how glorious Heaven must be...
no tongue nor pen can tell!

Psa.16:11   John 14:2-3

25

In the Beginning God

In the Beginning God was there.
Before He came forth,
naught did appear.
God, being with His Spirit, as also with His Son.
Before they'd manifested,
nothing had begun!
  First God decided
hence instantly declared, that He would make light...
by His Word—the light appeared!
  The light was called the day,
and the darkness He called night.
The firmament magnificent,
a sight of great delight!
And said it was good,
which meant it was right.
  The dry land from the seas
He caused to divide,
and every herb yielding fruit,
with its special seed inside.
  He made the stars also,
and the moon for a guide.
  Then in the seas, God conceived His latest feature;
there was found to abound ev'ry moving creature!
  Then the fowls He let fly,
commanded He now to multiply.
Then He said, "Ah, 'tis good!"
  And hung upon nothing,
there the World stood!
With cattle, horses, sheep in mind,
He made them also—after their kind.
  But one thing now did seem amiss...
With none was there to share all this.
So in His image made He man,
with whom God now could crown His plan;
who might love, enjoy and fill the land.
So made He Man!

 And with man to communicate,
from Adam's rib gave him a help-mate.
So in His image created Adam,
and gave to him a perfect Madam.
Therefore Eve was her name,
from whence all human beings came.
  So how it started, we can know,
God through His Word has told us so.
So, don't be monkeyed by "Darwinian fraud"---
But keep your faith in the living Lord!

Genesis 1:1   John 1:3

Not as Poor

Oh, think me not as being poor,
though fancy fads I've seldom wore.
Nor judge me by a humble shack,
God's presence there, I find no lack.
    I have no car.
A table, chair,
a bed to sleep in…
I owe much prayer!
    Though nothing's saved in any banks,
for Saving me…I give Christ thanks.
    I'm seldom hungry, cold or wet,
for God has never failed me yet.

Though in "man's view" I hold no rank,
what God gave me, I've much to thank:
for faith in Christ,
true peace of mind,
God's Love in Christ…
so hard to find.
And saved me…one deserving Hell,
what marvelous Grace, only Heaven will tell.

Don't think me poor, for I am not.
I thank the Lord for what I've got.

1 Tim.6:6

Some of life's greatest riches and treasures
--cannot be bought with money:
Life, true love, peace, good health and **Eternal Life in Christ!**

Thanks for the Gift

Dear friend to many—dear friend of mine,
whom countless lives you've touched.
Whose thoughts for others above yourself
pulled many from a clutch!
   God's 'gifted maestro'…the people's friend,
Heaven's music was your art—
yet equal gift, like sweetest music…
was your humble, loving heart.
   The many Christlike deeds you'd done—
in hearts shall never fade.
'Twas said by one, your special gift:
"Turning lemons to lemonade!"
   Your truly sound advice for Christ,
you taught me more than school.
For you dared to care and always share:
Encouragement was your tool!
   Your lovely music I still may hear,
a gift to you God gave,
but with the music God sent to us…
He lent us—Brother Dave.

Rev.14:13

From long time friend and beloved student,
to Bro. David E. Hanson, Choir Director,
"Grace Conservative Baptist Church"-Nanuet, N.Y. .
   "To be with Christ which is far better!"

AS LONG AS CHRIST STAYS IN THE BOAT

While storms of life might come and go,
Yes, here's a message you should know.
While fierce clouds threaten--
And high winds blow,
And there's no shelter nor port to go!
While tomorrow's promised to no man—
With things we just don't understand.
While life itself seems so uncertain,
While none can see beyond 'the curtain'.

Look unto Him, Who calmed the seas,
embrace His grace, get on your knees!
Consider Him when storms would rage—
Whose sweet voice fills the Sacred Page.
As with three words, He calmed the sea—
He'll do the same, for you and me.
And will sustain your bark afloat,
As long as Christ stays in the boat.

Matthew 8:26-27

"What manner of man is this?"

Be Not Deceived

No woman's heart can be that right,
While going 'round in slacks so tight!
"You've come a long way, Baby!"
the devil would say,
But God says there's coming a Judgment Day!
They think they've got such "sex appeal",
Not knowing 'how hot Hell Fire will feel'!
More men will be in Hell "by greater chance":
"Mini-skirts, low-necks, and skin-tight pants"!
Ol' Hellywood yells: "You're looking swell!"
Well, so did your mammy Jezebel!
Go ahead, keep getting "cutely dressed",
Without Christ in Hell...You'll be a mess!

Lk. 17:1
(There will probably be more men in Hell
because of the way 'many women are dressed **in
this generation**', than in any other generation.)
Jesus says in Luke 17:1" Temptations to sin are sure to come--
but woe be to the one through whom they come!" ESV

For whatsoever a person soweth that shall they also reap,
and they that sow to the flesh shall reap...corruption! Gal.6:7-8

"Preaching of the Cross" is Foolishness
to Them That are Lost

You say we preach too hard,
because you're really not of God!
That we make a lot of noise,
but you'll run with the foul mouth boys!.
Then you say there is no sin,
that's why Rape and Crime are in.
You think we preach too loud,
still you'll party with the "cursing crowd".
You would rather we not preach,
yet for Porn and trash you will reach!
The Preaching you'll evade,
So instead you'll get the herpes and the A.I.D.S..
You say 'we're not all there',
but tolerate the Mohawks and purple hair!
You say our preaching is too bold,
but around the corner drugs are sold.
You have the nerve to call us "fanatic",
but you won't give the mugger any static.
You refuse to take a Tract,
so instead you'll get the Crack.
You have no interest in the Lord,
so instead you'll get God's Sword.
Refuse the Gospel once too often,
there's no preaching in the coffin!
Love darkness, call God a liar,
You'll end up in the Lake of Fire!

1 Cor.1:18
*42nd St. N.Y.C. Street Preaching.1985

"I'd rather see a fool on fire than a scholar on ice!" Billy Sunday 1930

What Does It Profit?

There's the way of the World
which to man seemeth right,
as he tours through this life
with his short earthly sight.
Like sin's smoke screen of night-life,
its deceptions and dreams,
entertain the loud drunkard,
while the venomous vodka gleams.
The billboards, commercials,
T.V.'s plastic world sounds—
so alluring from "the boring"…
how delusion abounds!
For you see, sin, though shallow,
blinds the mind and runs deep,
not forthtelling the fact,
what one sows, one must reap.
If you sow to the spirit,
you'll reap Life that is true.
While also the flesh
must receive its own due.
What advantage is the temporal,
when one must pay **sin's** wage,
though your name blink in neon,
but…not inked on "**God's page**"!

Gal.6: 7-8

Life is short—Eternity long—sin the curse…
Christ the cure!

(ETERNITY IS TOO LONG TO BE WRONG!)

Dear Mr. Darwin:

Please don't make a monkey out of me,
Regardless of your million PhD's.
'Cause no aunt or niece of mine
ever gave birth to a 'gorilla kind'!
So don't try to make no monkey out of me!
Why don't you stop by at the local zoo,
And ask the O'rang-a-tang if he thinks
this "monkey business" might be true?
But I doubt if he'll agree,
(Since bananas are his specialty)
Though he may say: **"Hey dude, don't make
a human being out of me!"**
So please, don't make a monkey out of me,
Nor put a chimpanzee in my family tree!
You may hang by the gorilla coop,
But Sir, I'm from another group...
Please Mr. Darwin,
Don't try to make a monkey out of me!

Gen.1: 26   Col.2: 8

Don't let evolution make a Monkey out of you!
(Sorry, but I never saw any mother give birth to a gorilla or a chimp!)

The Miraculous Truth

Miracles—great wondrous acts
Which come from God alone.
As when He made both you and me,
Thus made His love be known.
How else was placed the Sun in space,
Great Planets…stars which hang;
Such vast Symphonic Galaxy,
Caused by a "Cosmic Bang"?
From dust of ground Creation's crowned,
In awesome wonder shaped:
Man's body, spirit, soul and mind
Were ne'er shared with the Ape!
Man tries to find out God through reason,
With fallen mind so small,
Which God thus capable of proof,
Would not be God at all!
And though the world cannot know God,
Mid sin—their hearts enticed,
Still no excuse could change this truth:
"What has one done with Christ?"
It matters not how 'Educated'—
Great intellectual wealth…
No man can search out God by Science,
By faith—reveals Himself!

From the wisest sage-philosopher,
to the bushman, far uncouth;
When each **repents and trusts in Christ,**
Both find "Miraculous Truth"!

1 Cor.2:14   Heb.11:13
  "But the things that are not seen are Eternal!"

Where Lies Thy Treasure

Where lies thy treasure,
Thy greatest care...
Would cause thy heart to shed a tear?
What things are they for which you toil:
earth's mammon, riches, fame and spoil?
To build up store or gain appeal,
where moths and thieves break in and steal?
Where lies thy heart's most valued price?
Is it this World, or is it Christ?
This life shall pass, its charms will fade,
the canker 'neath poised to invade.
But there awaits a Righteous Crown,
for those whose hope in Christ is found.
Life is not worth "gold's tinseled looks",
when God Himself opens the Books!
What is thy heart's most valued price?
Is it this World...or is it Christ?

Matt.6:19-21 and Mark 8:36

What shall it profit a man if he gains the whole world but loses his soul?

Paul the Apostle said: "I count all things rubbish
that I may gain Christ!"

It's Spring Again!

Nature dressed in vert array,

Adorns herself from day to day,

By quiet streams serene and gay.

With pastel roses, violets blue,

Pure lilies white with tint of dew

as colors clash with radiant hue.

Floating clouds 'neath sunshine's breeze,

Which sets the lustrous fields at ease,

As sparrows huddle 'neath budding trees.

As softening raindrops kiss the ground,

whence ripening, blossoming seeds are found,

The moonlight yields her silhouette,

The moment that the sun is set.

Her rainbow worn in such a way

As saying: "It's a happy day". . .

while butterflies begin their play!

Such perfumed fields so lush and green. . .

a winter's day has never seen.

Song of Solomon 2:11-12

36

While God Has Made the Eye

The fool hath said, "There is no God!"
What sad and hopeless thought!
Man's soul cries out, yea, longs for God!
Doth all resound of naught?
    Sweet fruit, bright blossoms, honeybees,
Roses' fragrant smells,
Majestic mountains, springs and fountains,
each gentle breeze compels.
    While sparrows sing, pure snowflakes cling
'neath sunsets' guilded hues.
Pure streams to drink, a mind to think,
Man's heart and will to choose!
    Yet, try to count each twinkling star
while treading woodlands wild.
Then muse into a microscope,
Or watch a newborn child!
    Or launch and search each galaxy's
vast planetary trail.
Then stand upon the mountain peak—
and watch the eagle sail.
    To stand and say, "There is no God!"
Your heart would tell a lie.
 Still man himself has no excuse--
While God has made the eye.

Romans 1: 20

The Fool has said in his heart—
"There is no God". Psa.14:1

Thus Saith the Fool

Who, but the fool says: "God is dead!"
If so...when did He die?
O, scores of skeptics, scholar-fools--
for decades vainly tried...
to disprove God, defame His Name,
or say "He'd met His end".
As Voltaire, Nietzsche, Ingersoll,
inspired by Satan's pen!
Can you conceive, these crawled from seas,
from trees swung by their tail...
whose great-great-grandson did descend,
is teaching now at Yale?
You see, the mind of humankind
is blinded by its sin.
Besides,"the god of this world"—Satan,
for men's souls tries to win!
Our battle's not against flesh and blood,
but "powers which are higher".
'Cause it's not God alone Who's real,
but Satan...who's a Liar!

Psalm 53:1

Atheism is not such an 'intellectual issue'
as much as it is a moral one!

JUDGMENT IS COMING

JUDGMENT IS COMING,
WHO WILL BE THERE?
THE SAVED IN CHRIST JESUS
SHALL BE CAUGHT UP IN THE AIR!
JUDGMENT IS COMING—
ALL WILL BE THERE!
JUDGMENT IS COMING,
THIS NATION WILL ACCOUNT.
THE BALANCE OF ITS SCALES
ARE FOUND WANTING—IN 'GREAT AMOUNT'!
IF SODOM HAD NO BIBLE,
AND NOAH'S DAY GAVE NO HEED,
WHO IS AMERICA...
FROM GOD'S WRATH SHALL IT PLEAD?
WE WHOM GOD HAS BLESSED GREATLY
AND CAUSED TO ABOUND,
WHO HOLD THE "TRUE GOSPEL",
WHAT EXCUSE WILL BE FOUND?
WHEN WE APPEAR BEFORE CHRIST,
AND OUR HARVEST BROUGHT TO LIGHT,
HOW SHALL OUR WORKS APPEAR IN HIS SIGHT?
WHEN THE CLERGY AND PROFESSORS
WHO WILL STAND BEFORE GOD,
WHO CALL EVIL GOOD, AND GOOD EVIL...
WHO THEN WILL SWALLOW HARD?
HOW DOTH HELL MOVE BENEATH THEE,
O, THOU DESPISER OF GOD'S WORD.
AND THE LAKE OF FIRE TURNETH OVER,
WHAT LAMENT SHALL BE HEARD!
YES, HELL HATH ENLARGED HERSELF,
 WHERE THE FLAMES NEVER COOL-
"BUT THERE IS NO GOD FOR ME",
 SAITH THE FOOL!
GOD'S JUDGMENT IS COMING,
MY FRIEND, DO NOT DOUBT,
FOR IN HELL THEY'LL CHECK IN-
BUT. . . .THEY'LL NEVER CHECK OUT!

Revelation 20:11-15

"It is appointed unto men once to die,
and after that the Judgment." Heb.9:27

39

Freewill

Freewill, God gives to man,
Allowing him to choose:
Obey or else to stray...
Man's will He'll not abuse.
God leaves the choice to man:
To wander or go straight.
Whatever choice he makes,
will so decide his fate!

Though lost Adamic man,
Would try—and try he would.
Without Christ in man's heart,
there's really nothing good.
While Heaven or Hell awaits
One's chosen destiny—
God left it in man's hands,
Where he'll spend Eternity!

Have you been Born Again—
Made Heaven your choice of home?
For Christ demands a choice,
even as you read this poem.

No choice is voting "No"!
From God you cannot hide.
Christ stands at the door and knocks,
while the latch is placed inside.

Rev.3:20
God did not make robots---but humans with an Eternal soul!

ETERNITY

ETERNITY, WHAT THOUGHT TIS MEANT,
WHERE ONE'S IMMORTAL SOUL IS SENT.
IF YOU HEAR GOD'S VOICE, TODAY REPENT,
LEST TOMORROW...LAMENT...FOR ETERNITY!
  "ETERNITY", SOUNDS EACH SECOND'S TICK,
NO START NOR END TO BURN THY WICK.
AND SOON SHALL PASS, HOW VERY QUICK
LIFE'S BREVITY...THEN ETERNITY!
  OUR LIVES ARE LIKE A VAPOR'S CLOUD.
ETERNAL TRUTH BY GOD IS VOWED.
BOTH GREAT AND SMALL,
EACH KNEE BE BOWED,
WHENCE ENTER IN.....ETERNITY!
  WHAT HOUR OF TRUTH WHEN TIME AND SPACE,
WHERE AT GOD'S THRONE, SHALL FIND NO PLACE.
BUT ONLY JUDGMENT THERE TO FACE,
THUS ENTER IN "ETERNITY"!
  ETERNITY, WHICH DESTINY IS MEANT,
EITHER HEAVEN OR HELL...
TO WHICH BE SENT...OH SOUL,
  IF YOU HEAR GOD'S VOICE, TODAY REPENT
LEST THOU LAMENT FOR. . . .ETERNITY!

Matt. 25:46

And as it is appointed unto man once to die and after that the judgment. Heb.9:27

The Bible says—"Behold now is the accepted time, behold now is the day of Salvation!" 2Cor.6:2

Pro-Choice is but Pro-Murder

They shout a woman's body
Belongs to her alone,
While countless unborn babies—
Into the trash are thrown!
I'm glad I was no fetus 'round 1989...
No poem would I be writing
if left in saline brine.
By mauling unborn infants,
"A woman's right," they say,
They justify their murdering
five thousand kids each day!
Pro-choice is but Pro-murder,
The surgeon loves his pay;
By mauling unborn infants...
Who'll never see the day.
Each poor defenseless infant—
A tiny human being:
With eyes and feet and heart beat...
His mom he won't be seeing.
He'll die a "clinic-killing",
A dangerous place to be.
Pro-murder was the Pro-choice,
Now his mom he'll never see.
They'll grab and yank his torso,
Then pierce his gasping throat,
Or poison him or torture her,
Just 'cause they cannot vote!
No animal would ever
Destroy its next of kin!
In man's eyes, "It's a woman's choice",
But in God's eyes, "It's sin"!
Thank God you were no fetus,
Once left in saline brine.
Your mother let you live,
So won't you be so kind?
Pro-choice is but Pro-murder,
America must pay.
Woe to the Bloody City
Upon that Judgment Day!

Jer.1:5 "Before I formed you in the womb I knew you."

How Can One Escape

Where might one escape—
When all around is sin,
Such as Noah's Day,
When evil seems to win!
Or how can one evade,
the Holiness of God,
When the final Gospel's preached,
And all flesh lies 'neath the sod?
And how shall one despise,
The Blood of Christ reject,
Whence told but otherwise,
Your eternal soul neglect!
Is there such escape?
Permit me now to tell;
Without Christ there's no escape,
The Eternal fires of Hell!

Hebrews 2:3

To Know He's There

Trust in the Lord, for trials are meant,
to show us surely—that He's our strength!
When all else falters…and life seems "odd",
what blest assurance, to know there's God!
Our source of strength—at times we're weak,
most faithful fortress, He's there to seek.
And thus the Spirit intercedes…
In all our trials, His Spirit leads.
With peaceful hearts, we've naught to fear--
what heartfelt joy. . .to know He's there!

Psa. 46:1
"And there is a friend that sticketh closer than a brother." Prov.18:24
"What A Friend We Have In Jesus"

43

They Took the Bible Out of School

They took the Bible out of school,
the Devil had a "field day".
He stormed right in, with sneering grin,
saying: "Now to run things my way!"
First to encamp, I'll hope to stamp
the Monkey as man's Uncle...Expel his Savior,
so his behavior and "music" match the Jungle!
I'll write the text for "intellects" to view the universe--
as just some 'giant Accident'
which ends once in the hearse!
To make him question moral values,
with fashions...keep him 'Mod'.
Teach "Sex-Ed.→Caution",
"Gay Rights", "Abortion",
while man will think he's God!
That there's no Judgment, men wrote the Bible,
no 'meeting of any Maker'.
Nor buy that 'fire and brimstone' stuff,
'cause the Preacher's a 'money raker'.
I'll bring in drugs, with pimps and thugs,
graffiti for free expression,
With 'Crack' and beer and Mohawk hair,
then pack a Guru Session.
Applaud his chosen new "life styles",
whatever they prefer.
If she would rather be a he,
so what...if he's a her?
And teach the word called "sin" is ancient,
man's thinking it retards.
(Now teachers dare not teach in schools
without Security Guards.)
They took the Bible out of school,
statistics wouldn't lie;
With all the cursing, AIDS and shootings...
the Public wonders why?
They took the Bible out of school,
yet kids can't add or spell.
They can't converse—unless they curse,
then scorn when warned of Hell.

Hell's hated rival is the Bible—
now look at "Education"!
Prayer and the Bible----expelled from School!
Sin's curse fell on this Nation!

Prov.14:34

To Hear None Swear Would Now Seem Rare

Was there once a time things got so bad,
When **obscene speech** became a fad?
Obscenities that stream the air...
To hear none swear **would now seem rare!**
When cursing and swearing seemed not wrong,
All **public ranks** have joined the throng.
From executives, policemen, **school-girls too,**
Can curse so bad—turn a sailor blue!
They can't express the thoughts they mean,
Unless they're speaking things obscene.
While **Rap and Hip Hop** spew such filthy words,
in my generation was never heard!
Who sense no guilt nor bit of shame. . .
With glib contempt, they use God's Name!
Their hearts and minds, their mouths so wreak,
The basest filth...no beast would speak.
Who think they're "macho", "hip", or brave,
Not knowing they're but Satan's slave!
And say they're "rappin"...what's happ'nin',
Yo, cool!
Each breath speaks death...a babbling fool!
Their vulgar lips and tongues insane,
God's Holy fury, such must attain.
God's Word, the Bible warns us well:
Though hushed the hearse...
They'll curse worse in Hell.

Romans 3:13-14 Jesus said: "that **every idle word** that men shall speak
they shall **give an account thereof** in the day of Judgment." Matt.12:36
(at least that's the pandemic it is here in "the Bronx and N.Y.C. area)

Jesus said: "From the abundance of the heart the mouth speaks."
Matthew 12:34-37
(P.S. According to Scripture. . . no one is getting away with anything!)

Whom We Serve

We serve a wondrous mighty God
who reigneth over all,
and said that He would answer us,
if on Him we would call.

Who hath all power in Heaven and Earth—
Thus, nothing's hard for Thee.
And by that Name above all names
We've got the Victory!

Just give us strength to serve Thee,
Grace to trust Thee all the while.
Faith to know that Thou art there,
to help us through each trial.

1 Thess. 5:24

God is big enough to rule the mighty Universe,
 yet small enough to live within one's heart!

When Christ the Righteous Judge Shall Rule

There is coming a Day of no sorrow nor pain,
when Brimstone alone shall be Satan's domain.
And sin shall no more be his tool;
When Christ the Righteous Judge shall rule!
  The end of all suffering, sorrows and woes;
except for Christ-rejecting sinners…
in the Lake of Fire---which they chose.
Yet victory through Jesus awaits the final duel--
when Christ, the Righteous Judge shall rule!
  The end of all evil, corruption and hate…
'cause no evil-doers shall enter that Gate.
Persecuted ones for the Gospel,
whom the World treated cruel,
shall then stand by Him in Victory,
Who in righteousness shall rule.
  What a great day is coming,
when the crooked is made plain,
whence the faithful reign with Jesus,
who have not wrought in vain.
  But unbelievers and deceivers
shall have their part as fuel,
where the worm dieth not,
and the flames never cool.
  When all time shall reach its peak,
and Christ shall seek His ransomed jewel--
The Blessed Word of God declares—
that Christ the Righteous Judge shall rule!

Cor. 15:24-26

P.S. Devil's goin' to da Lake a fire!

Alone With God

Spend time alone with God in prayer,
to get to know His voice,
so when life's tough decisions come—
they'll fall into His choice.
His Word will guide and give you peace
so you may know His will.
His special wealth and blessed health-
can curb the doctor bill!
Be bold by grace to seek His face,
Don't go by what you feel,
Trust and obey, for love's the way--
faith causes us to kneel.

James 5:16

Just Pray

When you don't know what to do—

With the storms you're going through,

Pray that God might have His way with you.

While life's pressures may surround,

And no answer can be found,

Lift your heart and soul to God and pray.

Oh, lift your heart and soul to God and pray,

So that God might have His way this day.

When the storms and trials bring

so much pain you cannot sing,

Lift your tears and cares to God and pray!

Psa. 57:1   Psa.120:1

There Is A Way

There is a way that seemeth right—
yet it leadeth straight to Hell!
With all the "Cults"…man-made religions,
which the Devil tries to sell.

For "Broad is the way, and wide the gate"—
that leadeth to despair!
And many, blindly are deceived,
who sadly enter there.

While Jesus told a group of Jews
who so rejected Him—
if they believed not Who He was,
they'd die still in their sin!

For there's no other way to Heaven,
except through Calvary—
for Jesus came to pay the price,
that we might be set free!

It's not by Mary, Mohammed, Buddha,
nor religion made by men.
But the Only Way to get to Heaven —
"One Must Be Born Again!"

Prov.14:12, Jn.3:3

49

Too Busy for God

The whole World seems like it's rushing so.
But where do people really go?
Some racing here and charging there,
yet many rush...not knowing where!
Must meet that dead-line by that date,
appointments such, while God can wait.
That must get finished, must do this...
my favorite program, I must not miss!
This I'll do, and afterwards,
I'll plan next week, count all my goods.

Running here and charging there,
no time for God, the Bible, prayer.
Just in earth's things his whole life spent,
no thought of God nor to repent.

But God said, "Halt!"
Still unretired, "This night thy soul shall be required!"
Whose things shall they be he once possessed?
Too busy for God, but not for death.

Luke 12:20

If you're **too busy** for God...then you **are too busy!**

The Peace of God

There's nothing like the peace of God
which comes from knowing Him;
Amidst life's storms and challenges,
wouldst faith and hope grow dim.
Still God's sweet peace stays pure and kind,
a touch of "Heaven's Care"--
A peace that passes understanding,
whence we've met God in prayer.
The roughest road that we'd ever tread—
the toughest load we'd bear. . .
But when He speaks: "Yea, peace be still."
the Risen Christ is near!
Such wond'rous peace, why would we forfeit,
or would we do with less—
when Jesus beckons to His children:
"Come unto Me and rest."
"My yoke is easy, My burden's light,
My Cross so justifies.
The living water and peace I give—
Within thy soul shall rise!"
O blest assurance—all sins forgiven,
no judgment need I dread,
And all because that wond'rous Cross
where Christ's own Blood was shed!

John 14:27 Col.1:20

Search Ye the Scriptures

"He came unto His own," says John,
though they received Him not.
Thus came the sinless Lamb of God,
without a stain nor blot.
With cruelty they treated Christ,
rejected and despised,
thus spake "Isaiah Fifty-three",
God's Son... unrecognized!
No room found Mary, though great with Child,
who made Him swaddling clothes.
God's Righteous Branch from dry ground sprang,
thence came up Jesse's Rose.

Thus entered Christ, God's Son to Earth,
to die and rise again.
Search ye the Scriptures,
Eternal Life is found in Bethlehem!
So do not stand with eyes made blind:
earth's cares, and ears thus sealed.
The Prophets' words are a Symphony...
to whom God's Son's revealed!

Isaiah 53:1

Many don't believe basically because....they don't want to believe...
which is really not an intellectual issue as it is a "moral one".
"Men love darkness rather than light because their deeds are evil."

May My Light Still Shine

Oh, may my light forever shine,
yet never once grow dim—
Bright and pure forevermore,
that others might see Him.
Yet might it glow, though troubles blow,
would winds of worry shake
the fervor of its glorious gleam,
with brightness overtake.

And while that snarlsome—wretched foe
enshrouds its tinselled frost,
to make this world so "brighter seem",
might brighter beam the Cross!
For what could hold a candle to
compare life's brevity…
midst sinful follies of this life
against Eternity!
And knowing that each single ray
reflects as Glory hath,
to grant to earth a brighter day,
which leads to Heaven's path.

So might Thy Light in me now shine
so ever fervently—
that might this world grow dark and cold…
I'll still shine bold for Thee!

Matthew 5:14-16

It's so **sad to hear** people say: " I used to go to Church when
I was younger, or....I once was a Christian or…I used to serve the Lord".

"Won't let Satan put it out, I'm gonna let it shine!"

The Power of Testimony

God changes lives, He changes hearts...
His Spirit touches souls!
No greater love can e'er be known,
the hardest hearts remolds.
Who but God can change a drunk,
make pure a profligate...
convert a convict on 'death row',
put love where once was hate?

From "alcoholic" to "Apostolic",
or drug fiend so obscene,
sin's lowest ranks to Jordan's Banks,
now stand the Lord's redeemed!

One might refute the Scripture's Truth,
and call the 'whole thing lies".
But who can argue face to face,
when a sinner testifies!

John 9:25   2 Cor.5:17

The strongest proof of the Bible, the Gospel and the existence
of God is a Christian's personal life and testimony!

And Let God's Peace

Why not be full of joy, dear heart,
as God would have you be?
Why not be filled with grace and peace—
with love and charity?
Why not permit the peace of God—
take rule within your heart?
Thus simply take God's 'Shield of Faith'
to quench doubt's fiery dart!

Decide to trust the Living God,
lay hold His Sovereign Grace,
and thus allow the Spirit's power
to find its healing place.

For God, the Son can lift us up,
Saying: Child, be of good cheer!"
and trust the One Who's overcome~
by faith believing prayer.
Col.3:15

Know Christ--know peace. No Christ-- no peace!

Speak Forth the Word

Speak forth the wondrous "Words of Life",
Christ's words of power let go!
Hence grace by faith cause to abound,
let streams of healing flow.
So speak Christ's Word, from Heaven brought
to us, His children's bread.
Send forth Christ's great transforming power
For which Christ's Blood was shed.
Still speak the Word, most precious Truth,
a bastion sent from Heaven,
true Victory, strength, purity
that purges out doubt's leaven.
A fount for cleansing, sword or fire,
a balm that grace reveals,
so speak the mighty Word of God,
which cleanses, soothes and heals.

2 Tim.4:2, Jn.6:63

If man's words have power. . . . consider the Word of God!

And God said: "Let there be light!"---
and there was light! Gen,1:3

Go Tell!

Awake ye Christians now!
Give head the trumpet call.
Received thou not God's blest command!
What causeth thou to stall?
Give heed the trumpet call!
Is not the hour late?
What hinders thou to go forth now
and change the sinner's fate?

Believest not there be a Hell?
Where Christless souls in torment dwell?
Hast thou not read where it is said
where Christ did speak of Hell?
But letting others perish soon,
whilst thou not go and tell?

Awake, thou slumbering heart,
let not each chance slip by.
"Had but thou warned me of this doom!"
Hear the lost's eternal cry.

Ezek.33:7

We are co-laborers with Christ! God decided to choose us, not angels, to carry out
the Good News of His Redemption Plan! And Jesus said: "Go ye into all the World
and preach the Gospel, and lo, I am with you always, even unto the ends of the
earth!" Mark16:15

Omniscience

God looks down upon His planet,
and always has, since He began it.
His thoughts transcend the deepest depths,
From stars to seas His footprint steps--
whence are His secret treasures kept.

He sees throughout all time and space;
past, present, future in one embrace--
can probe the myriad of Adam's race.
He knows our thoughts...our motives too!
Sees all we do from perfect view.
Thus knows who's false and knows who's true!
Who'll judge the evil, yet still gives hope.
Who dare approach such endless scope,
nor yet compare their minds so small—
to God above, Who knoweth all!

Psa. 44:21 Rom.2;16 Acts::15:15

"Known onto God are all His works from the beginning."
He knew us even before we were born!
He's Almighty, all knowing and all loving God! Amen.

Trust God

The Lord is good.
He knows our need.
This is God's Word
We gladly read.
He cannot fail,
Nor can He lie,
For He will answer...
Bye and bye.
Though roads and mountains
We must climb,
We know we shall
Arrive on time.
We can embrace
His plenteous Grace,
If in His Word
Our trust is placed.
We must stand strong
'til trials are gone,
And shall rejoice
that we've held on!
So do not fret—
God's Word is true,
And don't forget...
He still loves you.

Jer.29:11

The most important thing God wants--
is that we trust Him!

Thanksgiving Prayer

We thank Thee Lord for all Thy gifts;
Thy mercy, love divine:
The sun, the stars, the wind, the rain—
For all of these are Thine.

But great is our forgetfulness,
As once a year we say—
Our thanks to you for all you do,
Just on Thanksgiving Day!
But truly Lord, our hearts are grateful.
For little do we lack.
For all the things which Thou didst give…
Not one can we in turn give back.

We're thankful for our eyes and ears,
Our body, mind and soul,
Our hands and feet…
the food we eat,
a shelter from the cold.

For family, friends and loved ones dear,
the love we share in Thee—
For opening up our Spiritual eyes,
So that we might now see!
And thank Thee for Salvation's Gift—
The Gospel Message free!
But most of all we're thankful that…
Someday we shall see Thee!

Psa. 100:4

Most of all, besides our trust, God desires--
our appreciation and gratitude.

Praise God from Whom all Blessings flow!

An Evergreen

O wonderous Tree—

thy blessed sight-

Now huddled in the starlit night!

O Christmas Tree, thy liberty-

 dispels the blight of tyranny.

Such beauteous boughs of evergreen,

More peaceful sight was rarely seen.

Thy faithful leaves unchanging true—

bring faith and hope the whole year through!

O Christmas tree so fair and free;

You are God's wond'rous gift to me.

Though once a year you dress so bright,

and bring to many great delight!

Blest Christmas tree, yea might I see

 what blessed joy you bring to me!

Your leaves unchanging represent—

the Gift unchanging God has sent!

Your timeless spirit and grace so true,

Uphold the Star we place on you.

O wond'rous Tree with Star so bright--

Adorns the Blessed Christmas night.

Thanks For Christmas

We thank Thee God for Christmas,

though coming once a year,

Brings love, hope and gladness,

with Blessed joyous cheer!

Now thank Thee God for Christmas,

No day has greater worth.

For then was marked that special time

Salvation came to Earth!

Though Satan was defeated,

yet still he fights that Day!

But regardless of his tactics,

this Day has come to stay!

It's CHRISTMAS, never X-mas, nor Happy Holidays,

for its greatness and its Glory

deserve the highest Praise!

Matt.1:21

To Whom Honor Belongs

What joy and happy-merriment
One's tongue can hardly speak,
Which might describe the Christmas-Time,
That fine December week!
Might 'words' bestow such 'glorious glow'
To show the Love of Him,
Who opened Heaven's Gates of Grace,
In lonely Bethlehem.

So many songs and poems and paintings—
Seem their theme grows tired,
But none stays fresher year to year
As Christmas keeps inspired!

It's not because of lighted trees,
Nor parties, gifts nor songs,
But all because of Jesus Christ,
this Blessed Day belongs.

Luke 2:10

God deserves our honor and respect, for where would we be today
had He not visited Earth--- born of the Virgin Mary in that humble
town of Bethlehem?

P.S. I truly doubt that there would ever be a country called
the United States of America, had not Christ come to earth,
neither would there have been a civilization as we know today!

The Meaning of Christmas

What wond'rous grace...
He took my place
When Christ in flesh descended.
Was born to die upon a cross—
The breach of sin be mended.
Beneath that Star in a manger lay,
Yet with a cross in view.
The reason for the Season was
To die for me and you.

It is not Santa, mistletoe,
That make the Season bright—
But that the Savior came that we...
With God might be made right!

1Tim.1:15
Christ became the Son of man that we might become the sons of God.

Bethlehem's Gift

As Christmas time has come again,
we turn our thoughts to Bethlehem.
So great Salvation came that day,
all cuddled in a crib of hay!
No miracle could e'er compare
with the gift which Mary
so did bear.
Which prophets spake in centuries past,
thence did appear God's gift at last!
O Bethlehem, thou humble place,
where God did send His gift of grace.

Gal. 4:6 But when the fullness of time was come,
God sent forth His Son, made of a woman,
made under the law, to redeem them that
were under the law.

A Steward's Blessing

I am so blest to know the Lord.
I have a heart to love my God.
I have two hands to give to those
who are in need of food and clothes.
I have a mouth to speak for Him,
To point the world away from sin.
I have two ears to hear His Word,
I have His grace when hope's deferred.
I've got two eyes, two feet a nose,
to walk and see and smell a rose.
I have a message from the Lord
So others' lives might be restored.
I have a life to live for Him;
I have a chance for souls to win!
I have a smile, a Savior true,
A home in Glory. . .and so can you!

Matt. 20:28   Matt.25:42-46
Dedicated to "Grace & Hope" Missionary women, Manhattan, N.Y.C.,
where for ten years volunteered. Also to Franklyn Graham's "Samaritan's Purse".

We are commissioned to be God's hands, feet and voice, (ambassadors)
 through the Holy Spirit...for we are **saved to serve**. . .the Lord!

If I Might Help

I thank You Lord for using me,

'tis by Your strength divine--

for all the talents, time and treasure

are truly only Thine!

For giving help and sustenance

to those who can't afford;

You said by giving those in need

is like lending to the Lord.

The goods I have may be but few,

my treasure may be small,

but little is much when God is in it

Whose bounty blesses all!

When I was hungry, naked, in prison—

Or on my way to Hell,

wouldst thou but ever hesitate--

The Gospel News to tell!

It's but a privilege to serve the Lord-

to represent The King!

'Cause when You gave Yourself to me,

You gave me everything!

Matt.25:25-35

Rejoice, Give Thanks

Lift high your heads—
ye Saints of God!
Rejoice amidst His Grace!
And dwell upon His wondrous love,
His joy would light thy face.
Rejoice ye Saints, look unto Him...
forget the thing you feel,
Go by the Word of God itself,
for God, His Word are real!
Then seek to serve thy fellowman,
be thankful every day.
Then meditate upon the Word,
and don't forget to pray.

Rejoice ye Saints, and think of Heaven,
for you Christ did prepare.
Recall all Christ has done for you,
then why would you despair?

O, love the Lord and give Him thanks,
though times. . .life may seem hard!
For all things work together for good
To those who trust in God.

Romans 8:28

I Know

I know that Jesus loves me,
He told me in His Word.
He cares for you, He loves you too—
in case you haven't heard!

He watches o'er me day and night—
I know I'm in His care,
And when I wish to give him "thanks",
I'll just send up a prayer.

Though days seem long and weary,
And some may oft seem bleak,
He's still my joy, my hope my strength,
Though times my faith grows weak!

But just remember—He is God,
And God is love indeed.
No matter where
the road might veer—
His love shall safely lead.

1 John 4:10

To know the love of Christ--
gives life its greatest meaning!

Trinity in Salvation

Blest Trinity, what mystery,
the Father, Spirit, Son...
had dwelt together, separate never—
before time had begun.
Whence ages past, eternity,
thence knowing what would be,
the Son agreed to intercede
and go to Calvary!
The Father leading, the Spirit pleading
Deliverance by the Word,
Who did descend to Bethlehem,
what "Wond'rous Grace" occurred!

Divinity in harmony, and unity in each,
whilst God did send His Son to mend
lost man's Adamic breach.

The Father thought it,
the Son had brought it,
the Spirit taught it plain:
"Redemption" body, spirit, soul,
whence being 'Born Again'.

Blest Trinity in Unity,
what wond'rous revelation!
The Father, Son, and Spirit one,
co-worked in man's Salvation.

1 Tim.3:16
Try to figure it out—you could lose your mind!
But (to refuse to believe it—you will lose your soul!)

Too Late

Before the Almighty—there stood a mortal
at the Judgment Hour.
And trembled as he stood alone,
possessed he not a power.
And God had looked upon his face,
as though His eyes would say:
"Did not I call thee more than thrice,
Yet thou didst go thy way?"
And echoed through his feeble mind,
it seemed as though just then,
he'd heard the Pastor's invitation—
time and time again!
And looking back it seemed as though
his life was but a day.
And all the things he lived his life for--
all had passed away!
In silent shock, he utterred nothing. . .
but stood without a hope nor mortal plea.
And being not found in "The Book of Life"
he cried and cried pitifully...
"My God, my God, have mercy, he cried;
What is there to do?
If I could even give my life,
For one last chance, but to make it through!"
Without another word then spoken,
the Mighty Wrath upon him fell...
So doomed was he--that it might be his soul. . .
Eternity in Hell!

Luke 16:23

There's a Hell to shun and a Heaven to gain.
The Eternal choice is given to each of us by God.

By trusting His Grace

I thank You Lord for saving me,
with gratitude I'll tell,
how I received a home in Heaven,
whence I deserved but Hell.
Amazing, how You called me out,
chose me to be Your own—
by merely just receiving Christ,
and trust His Grace alone!
I could not merit, work nor earn
a place in Heaven blest—
but only through Christ's sacrifice,
with heart and mouth confessed.

I shall look back midst ages hence—
through eons I shall gaze,
and thank You Lord for Saving me...
with gratitude I'll praise.

So might this message which I write,
Be read by one and all,
and trust the Gospel of Thy Grace--
and on Christ's Name would call!

Titus 3:5

If you're **one of the blest** who responded to Christ and are on your way to Heaven, consider it **most blest**! For many will not make it! It's all by **the grace of God**... so prepare your heart to be a bearer of **"God's Good News"**! As a nobody, telling everybody, about Somebody....Who can save anybody!

Sing Me a Song About Jesus

Sing me a song about Jesus,
Sing of His wonderful love.
Tell of His marvelous power to save,
Coming from Heaven above.
Sing me a song about Jesus,
Sing of His riches untold.
Tell it so joyously,
Sing it so gloriously,
Sing of the Savior I love.

Tell me the Heaven-sent Gospel,
Shepherds and prophets foretold.
Tell me the "good news" that angels can't sing—
The message that never grows old!

Tell me the great truth unshrouded:
God manifested in flesh!
Give me the History
And unfold the mystery—
Sing me that song I love best.

Col.3:16

" No sweeter sound than Thy blest Name,
O Savior of mankind!"

The Power of the Tongue

That "little thing", known as the tongue—
has such amazing power—
Can make one's whole day either sweet,
or else can make it sour.
Can turn the heart of men or kings
to peace or else to war.
And rarely does it cross one's mind
what power it has in store.

The Bible says: "God spake the Word",
and thus the Worlds were formed.
Christ raised up Lazarus by His Word,
then stilled the raging storm.

Christ is the Word Who always was,
Who took on human flesh...
That all who would believe His word,
would never taste of death.

In similar way, God gave man power:
to curse or else to bless—
Thus carefully must we watch our tongue,
or get what we confess.

Prov.18:21

Jesus said:"By thy words ye shall be justified and
 by thy words ye shall be condemned!"
Matt.12:36-37

The Bible

The Bible, written by men of God
moved by the Holy Ghost:
Disciples, Prophets, Kings and shepherds,
Elect, anointed host.
From "In the beginning God created,"
to "God so loved the World",
and all the way to Revelation…
out-values choicest pearls.
For in it rests the dearest treasure,
which can't be bought nor sold;
for here the truth of God's great Love
within its pages hold!
What Book Divine, God's mind revealing,
on its pages lie. . .
from Christ to sin and all within--
transcending from on High.
God's very breath which shaped the Worlds,
and formed man's living soul,
springs forth from deep within God's thoughts,
each word of truth unfolds.
Which sound sends life to all Creation,
having heart or ear,
to make the simple wise in Jesus,
which such He loves to share.

For in the Bible God is speaking
what He would to you.
Not just in life, but after death
will prove God's Word is true.

2 Tim.3:16
"I believe **the Bible** is the greatest **gift** God has ever given to man.
All the good from the Savior is communicated through this Book."
Abraham Lincoln

74

As Did David

Though none shouldst delve into the battle
as David did of old...
defiant giant, he withstood,
through God, waxed David bold.
Asked, "Who's this fiendish Philistine
which speaks his curse abroad,
displays his vile despising wit
at the "Armies of the Lord?"
Thus bold in spirit, sling in hand,
stepped forth in crucial plight.
Still greater truth should indicate,
transcended David's might.
Now gruesome giant, spear in hand,
intimidates with sword,
undaunted David, five smooth stones
proclaimed his faithful Lord!
For when the stone that David hurled
had reached its new abode,
God's great and sovereign omnipotent might
Without a doubt was showed!
So likewise such in power anointed
Thus by God's Spirit we,
can go forth bravely into battle,
defeat the Enemy.
Yet don't forget, as David didn't,
God's Armor, not earthly viewed,
but only with the Word of God
and through His Spirit endued.
With Jesus as our Armor bearer,
and Captain of His Host;
not by our power nor by our might
hath flesh no place to boast.
Today there strive 'Goliath Forces',
especially in this Age,
whence only dare we win the 'Battle',
God's Weapons we engage.
2 Cor.10:3-5

If Only

I know my life would be alright,
If I just walk within the Light.
My fears and worries all would fade—
If I but only stopped and prayed.
I know all things would be O.K.,
If I just took the time to pray.
And called upon the "One Who Can",
Who holds the planets in each Hand!
And then my life would all be fine,
If with the Master I would dine.
Then shall my life be one of faith—
And live as "Hebrews-Eleven" saith.
O, keep my mind in perfect peace,
And help me Lord, my faith increase.

Isa.26:3

Pray....God is listening!
 For we walk by **faith** and not by sight.

To Know He's There

Trust in the Lord, for trials are meant,
to show us surely—He is our strength!
When all else falters...and life seems "odd",
what blest assurance, just knowing God!
Great source of strength--when we are weak,
most faithful fortress, so might we seek.
And thus the Spirit intercedes...
In all our trials, His Presence leads.
With peaceful hearts, we've naught to fear--
what blessed joy. . .to know He's there!

Psa. 46:1
 "And there is a friend that sticketh closer than a
 brother." "What A Friend We Have In Jesus"

K.J.V.   (sung to the tune of "Old Time Religion")

(Dedicated to all King James Onlyers)

(Chorus)

O give me that King James Version,
give me that King James Version,
It has brought such blest conversions,
and it's good enough for me.
It was good enough for Wesley, It was good for Dwight L. Moody,
Seemed so right for Charles Finney, and it's good enough for me.
Give me that King James Bible, it has brought such great revivals,
you can keep its other rivals, yes, it's good enough for me!
It was good for William Boothe, and when Spurgeon preached the Truth,
though some say they want more proof,
still it's good enough for me.
It was good for Hudson Taylor, how those missionaries tarried,
David Livingstone, William Carey and it's good enough for me.
It was good for George Mueller, it was great for Charles E Fuller,
it was fine for Billy Sunday and it's good enough for me!
It was good for George Whitefield, as it stood by
Johnathan Edwards, George Washington, Daniel Webster--
and it's good enough for me.
Those great Pilgrims came before ya, Abr'ham Lincoln, Queen Victoria,
Isaac Watts and Fanny Crosby and it's good enough for me.
It was good for C.I. Schofield, Wigglsworth and Billy Graham,
John R. Rice and R. A.Torrey and it's good enough for me.
Pilgrim's Progress it inspired, as was **Handel's loved "Messiah"**,
and it still has plenty of fire, yes it's good enough for me.
So give me that **King James Version**,
give me that King James Version,
it has brought such blest conversions
and it's good enough for me.
So gimme that King James Bible,
it has brought **such great Revivals,**
you can keep it's other rivals,
still it's good enough for me!

Jer.6:16

The KJV is the most sacred, majestic, time tested, powerful, anointed, literary treasure that has caused great revivals, encouraged missionaries and is quoted more than any book. .

Ode to Christmas

How Sacred are thy Sounds—O Christmas,
How fragrant, warm and sweet.
No sonnet sung so rapturous,
the ear did ever meet!

With charming bliss, so sonorous,
thy hallowed praise 'tis shown.
Celestial sounds thy glory crowns,
as harps and horns intone.

Its trumpets tell thy blessed joy,
ne'er known to beast nor brute,
Of "Something" loftier than life,
with organ, voice and flute.

Now Christmas Sing, thy bells now ring,
with charming grace be strong.
How Sacred are thy Sounds, O Christmas,
For Jesus is thy Song.

Luke2:11

Consider First the Price

It costs to follow Christ in service,
which may mean sacrifice.
As Jesus said to follow Him,
consider first the price!
To live for Him, the flesh must die,
self yields, takes up the Cross.
Christ becomes the Master now,
no longer self the boss.
"For me to live is Christ", said Paul,
"and dying would be gain".
Is He the Lord of all your life,
does Christ have total reign?
Yet many Christians claim loftily
how Jesus they love grand,
but when the time for action comes,
would dare they take their stand?
Would they keep still and meek at sin,
not warning to repent,
are they ashamed of Jesus' name...
social embarrassment?
Ashamed of Christ, the Word of God,
He'll be ashamed of you,
and stand before the Son of God,
when this brief life is through.

Some Christians see the Christian life as
only sweet and nice,
but Jesus said to follow Him,
consider first the price.

Mark 10:21-23

Weep Not

Oh, do not cry for me,
I've reached a better place.
and neither wish me back—
for I have run 'the race'!
Nor think upon my pain,
nor pity should thou borrow.
But look now unto Christ,
be not like those who sorrow.
The great transaction's done!
The soul in Christ doth hide.
Since now my trust was placed,
in Him---the Crucified!
But rather weep for those
who've shunned the Savior's plea.
Consider now their fate…
for all eternity!
Might I more blessed be,
nor seek a better place,
than present with my Lord,
to thus behold His face.

For all which I had sought,
had longed and dreamed and planned,
at last I've entered in,
and reached that Haven Land!

2 Cor.5:6-8,

Bro.Izzy (present with the Lord)
We have this hope---we shall see our loved ones again!

He That Watches Israel

He that watches Israel doth slumber not
nor sleep—
But watches ever, day and night,
from hills to valleys deep.

While watching over Jordan's banks
to guide its fairest flow,
still sees the pilgrim pon'dring 'pon
the path of Jericho.
And hears a lost sheep's bleating cry,
then lifts him in His arm,
And leads them unto pastures green,
by quiet streams so calm.

Who hears a cry and follows by,
when one but faintly calls.
Not hair nor feather of a sparrow
without His knowledge falls.

God watching over Israel,
still watches by and by,
Doth never sleep, but ever keeps
with loving watchful eye.
.
Psa.121:4

Some proof of God's existence is:
Creation and 'the survival of the Jew'!

Ecclesiastes

What sighs the Preacher...
"'Tis all but vain?"
Refrains: "What is life for?"
The eye and ear seem never full,
yet ever wanting more.
Pond'rous sages fill vast pages
with 'wisdom' truly great.
Yet not a single new solution
to solve man's 'cyclic fate'.

For though one were to 'gain the world',
but then—were death to call!
And so when asked...how much he left?
"They say, he left it all!"

So having all earth's fame and riches...
even as Solomon did,
yet live and die a Christless life,
would prove a hopeless bid.

For nothing in this mortal life,
bar none-- how rich nor smart,
can satisfy the soul as Christ,
nor fill man's empty heart.

Matt.16:26

For we have brought nothing into this world
and for sure, we can take nothing out.

It's been said: "No one has ever seen a U-Haul
being pulled by a hearse!

Deity with Capital "G"

God was manifested in the flesh…
God, spelled with capital "G".
Mere carpenter of Nazereth?
Changed History to A.D.!
God in the flesh was manifest,
"The Word with God being God."
That Heaven-sent priceless, sinless Lamb,
to Heal a World sin-scarred.

Yes, God in the flesh made Manifest,
by Virgin birth came He.
The Word with God, still very God…
The greatest mystery!
All things which are were made by Him.
Less Christ, was nothing made;
Else by His Life might Calvary yield
Hell's ransom "Fully Paid"?
Vast multitudes He healed and fed,
then calmed the stormy sea.
From the tombs awoke, death's shackles broke,
spoke of His Deity.
Those who in darkness once had sat,
arose to Heaven's light.
And those who chose His path arose,
forgiven in His sight!
The Word as God now dwelt with men,
Still His own received Him not.
But once His Message they believed,
Eternal Life they'd got.
Christ became man, died and revived,
so dwelt and felt as we.
Who then was Manifest in the Flesh?
But God…with Capital "G"!

Jn.1:14

God Never Changes

God does not change—Great Mighty Rock.
Let heathen rage—the godless mock.
Would planets plummet, high mountains fall,
God Who's our Refuge, reigns over all.
He varies never, so kindly sweet,
in Prayer, who beckons, his need He'll meet.
From age to age, each generation,
in loving Grace, shows His Salvation.
Will ne'er revoke His Promise Grand:
thy soul eternal…kept in His Hand!
The Master's Name upholds His Seal,
each tongue confess and knee shall kneel.

World's suns shall dim, seas cease to roar,
Christ still our Anchor—
standeth sure.

Mal.3:6

God is omnipotent, omniscient, omnipresent and immutable!
He is also love! Awesome!

Thy Merciful Care

While I'm pleading which I pray for—
Grant Thy leading, Blessed Savior.
By Thy mercies I am blest...
Knowing that Thy way is best!

Hide me in the Rock of Ages-
even as the tempest rages.
While my life seems going down,
Help me reach Heaven's Higher Ground!

Teach me Father as You would,
Knowing that it's for my good.
 My soul, my life, my body mend,
Jesus, Savior, Counselor, Friend.

1 Pet. 5:7

A Simple Morning Prayer

Thank You Jesus for today.

Help me now to watch and pray...

That ev'rything might go Thy Way. . .

And guide me lest I go astray,

And in my heart I hope You'll stay--

ev'ry moment. . . ev'ry day.

Heb.13:5b

If I'll But Tarry Still

When e'er I'm in God's will,
With joy my heart is filled!
While casting ev'ry care—
Upon my Lord in Prayer.
When I do what He bids me do,
And His Grace shall see me through—
His Word becomes my quest,
And know His way is best!
When He is my Delight,
And strive to do what's right,
My doubts and cares He lifts,
Then sends with blessed gifts.
I'll not be moved by ill,
While instead His Presence thrills.
With Assurance shall abide—
A precious Heavenly tide.
If I'll but tarry still,
To do God's Perfect Will.

Psa. 27:14
To do God's will is basically to trust His Word and to wait on Him in Prayer!
(Although honestly, waiting patiently on God may be one of the harder tasks
in the Christian's life.)

By Sculpturing Hand

I thank you Lord for loving me
with all that You have sent—
to bless and teach that I might reach
the "purpose" which You have meant.
With "trials to temper", teach and test,
allow in "retrospect",
to ever view, what I've gone through
was not done by neglect.

I'd thank You for each lesson given,
so learn them as I must,
that keeping with Thy Providence,
I've learned to hope and trust.
I thank You for such trying things,
as an oyster "pearls the sand"...
for pleasant ways, or rainy days,
that came by Sculpturing Hand.

Rms. 8:28

"If you live a holy life, shun the wrong and do the right, I know the Lord
will have His way with you!"   (Old Gospel chorus)

The Steps of a Good Man

The man of God who lives by "faith",
Is counted "being just",
If faithful to his Master's will,
And in His Word doth trust.

And though he might err seven times...
By Grace he finds his "Poise",
Stays "tuned in" to His Master's Voice,
Discerned from other "noise".

On 'narrow track'...would not look back,
trusts God's Word and is wise,
Then lifts his eyes unto the hills,
And face unto the skies.

"The Steps of a Good Man by God are Led",
Is what the Scriptures say,
And what he does shall please the Lord,
Who delighteth in His way.

Psa.37:23

"Walk with the King and be a Blessing!"

A Wedding Poem

Trust in the Lord with all of thy heart.
Trust Him, and fret not thy soul.
His gracious Hand will bind as love's hand.
His kindness fulfill all His plan.

Trust in the Lord, none greater joy.
He is the giver of peace.
He hath redeemed, forever will keep.
He giveth His life for His sheep.
Trust in thy God, thy union He'll bless.
Goodness and mercy are thine.

Love suffereth long,
is gentle and kind, not envious,
nor seeketh her own.
It thinketh no ill,
is pure,
and hopes still,
abideth, and shall never fail.

Trust in the Lord, His love will guide.
Some day He'll come for His Bride.

Prov.3: 5-6

1Corinthians Chapter 13 is probably the greatest treatise—
definition of love ever expounded!

God Is Love

Love soars above man's highest thoughts,
Not found in books nor tales,
it can't be conjured, fashioned, bought,
whereof, true love is real.
The word itself 's a theme for volumes,
notions oft untrue,
whence usually almost every person
has a different view.
Though love is tender, dear and precious,
one might call divine,
can stir the heart-felt inner depths--
with joy or else to pine.
It makes 'life's theater' liveable,
each act of hope completes,
brings meaning, purpose, zest to life,
and sings above defeats.
It ever gives, thinks not to take,
hopes but the other's good,
endears all things and bears all things…
sometimes misunderstood.
Sublimest word and dearest thought
the human tongue could prod,
if that one word might be defined--
that one word might be "God"!

1John 4:8

"…but the greatest of these is love!"

The Bride of Christ

How resplendent is the Bride of Christ,
Adorned with diamonds bright.
Whose pristine gleams—heavenly grandeur,
seems to meet the King's delight.

Her countenance glistening eyes of love,
lips of grace and peace.
Such dear, eternal, noble gift
wouldst never find decease.

So splendid stand her doors of truth,
the Gospel for her veil;
Whilst Christ the Chiefest Cornerstone,
All Hell durst not prevail!

Her dowry purchased dearest worth,
the Blood of God's own Son.
Her robes made white, His precious Blood,
Love comparable to none.

How lofty her beauty,
how fragrant her spice,
how dear the finest gem,
When Christ returns to rapture
His immortal diadem.

Rev.21:2

Marriage is a symbol of Christ and the Church,

Just in Christ Abiding

All my faith's in Christ abiding,
Not once in device nor deed,
but the Spirit now residing.
Thy dear blood meets all my need.
Blessed Jesus, only Savior,
God of love, Friend above.
Ever drawing now imploring,
with Thy precious matchless love.

Ever trusting in Thy fullness,
as Thy Spirit now indwells,
Ev'ry doubt and wayward spirit
Thy most blessed Word dispells.
Draw me closer to Thy Fountain,
so to cleanse from my self-will,
that I might now hear Thee calling,
Thy pure voice, so dear and still.

Jn.15:4

"And the voice I hear as I tarry there…
none other has ever known.

Faith

Faith is but a gift of God,
God gave for us to use,
that's sent to ev'ry Christian's heart,
to exercise or lose!

Faith holds the Key to Victory
Which opens up Hope's Door,
but not unless it's exercised,
might God e'er grant us more.

By Grace through faith we come to God,
by faith His will fulfill.
And so by faith. . .Heaven is our Home,
by faith we're waiting still!

Without Faith, one cannot please God—
nor enter Canaan's Land,
nor ever grow as unto Christ--
nor live within God's Plan.

Heb.11:6 Hab.2:4

We can only know, please, and walk with God by faith.
 For the righteous shall live by faith!

Abraham

Abraham believed His God,
his fervent heart was beckoned.
His sins were covered by God alone,
his righteousness--God had reckoned.

Such ne'er achieved through works that flesh--
born by his will to get.
For such a righteousness so earned,
would not prove grace but debt.

Thus Abraham, God's faithful friend,
God's promise ne'er refuted.
And so received His Righteousness
God sovereignly imputed.

He held respect, God's recompense,
his body though infirm,
still staggered not, but knew through faith—
God's Word would be confirmed!

So steadfast anchored on that Rock,
he'd overcome doubt's storm.
And was persuaded, what God had promised,
He surely would perform.

Was not by keeping 'Sinai's Law',
the Heart of God ungrieved.
By simple faith was justified,
God's Covenant he received!

So birthed the faith of Abraham,
the cost of faith, love's price.
So by God's Grace we're Justified,
God's gift...the Cross of Christ!

So when we trust in Jesus Christ,
God's sin-Atoning Lamb,
Heav'n's Gates are wide, being Justified,
with faithful Abraham.

Gal.3:16 His faith was counted unto him for righteousness!
Romans 4:5 Now to him that worketh not but believeth on Him
that justifieth the ungodly, his faith is counted as righteousness.

That He Should Make of Me

As Jesus gave His life for me,
I vow to give to Him:
my life, my all, my heart's full love--
by Grace, shall ne'er grow dim!
If He would condescend to earth,
hence leave all Heaven's store,
then how can I withhold earth's gold,
wouldst not I render more?
My plea shall be that He would take my will
and make of me,
at least the Shadow of the Form
Who hung on Calvary's tree.
For now that I in full, clear view,
so deeply know the truth,
the more I enter into it,
I want no substitute.

Gal. 2:20

"To know Jesus is to know God, and to know God
is to have Life Everlasting." John 17:3

A Stranger Still?

A 'Stranger' stepped into a boat,
with words so graciously spoken.
The common people all drew near:
 the lame, the blind, the broken.
There trod the poor, the lepers came,
such wounded souls drew near.
Miraculous deeds and 'Words of life'
they were to see and hear!
Such parables as: "the loving Shepherd",
whose lost sheep sadly roamed---
The 'Priceless Pearl', 'The Unjust Judge',
 a Prodigal son left home.
 These "timeless truths" fell from His lips...
from whence such knowledge came?
Yet all around the crowds grew large,
thus spread this Stranger's fame!
A woman groped to touch His cloak,
by doctors she grew worse.
But she touched the hem of His garment when,
At last--thus broke the curse!
The blind-man saw, the deaf did hear,
He even raised the dead!
He bid the raging storm, "Be still!",
then 'multitudes' He fed!
His enemies came to seize Him once,
and do as were commanded,
but when they heard the words He spake...
they went back empty-handed!
"None ever spake as did this Man!"
To harlots, outcasts, lame!
To those nobody cared about,
yet He sought no wealth nor fame.

With envy they crucified the Lord...
 that to Hell we need not go.
'Twas not that we deserved such love--
But because He loved us so.

They nailed this 'Stranger' to a cross,
where on Golgotha's mount,
the sins of every human soul
were placed to His account.

This 'Stranger's' not a stranger now,
 stays near me where I go.
And by my love and faith in Him,
 Eternal Life I'll know!
Is He a 'Stranger' yet to you. . .
 Your soul cannot afford.
So why not let this 'Stranger' be
your Savior and your Lord?

"He came unto His own and His own received Him not, but to as many as received Him
 gave He power to become the sons of God, even to them that believe on His Name." John 1:12

Only Jesus

Only Jesus can satisfy the soul,
Only Jesus can ever make you whole.
Only Jesus can take away your sin.
Only Jesus, can offer peace within.
Only Jesus, can catch the falling tear.
Only Jesus, might all your sorrows bear.
Only Jesus can give you life anew.
Only Jesus, can give you love that's true.
Only Jesus, can hear you while you pray.
Only Jesus, can lift your cares away.
Only Jesus, each pressing case defend.
Only Jesus can keep you 'til the end.
He won't vanish, when life's hour strikes "Eleven",
Only Jesus, can bring your soul to Heaven!
Of ten thousands, there is none that is so fair.
 Who with Jesus, can anyone compare?

Col. 2:10

How I Remembered My Jewish Dad

I wasn't with you dad, in your last days,
but God was with you dad...always.
From the time you found that New Testament...
in that dresser-drawer, you were sure--
God's Son was sent!

Your heart found a joy, your voice found a song.
Though raised a Jew in Brooklyn,
you knew the Rabbis were wrong!
That joy burned within, and had to come out--
that Jesus is the Messiah,
beyond the shadow of a doubt!

From the streets to the missions, where handing out tracts...
the testimonies, the preaching,
the Gospel, "a life changing fact"!
You pleaded with the Jews,
with street hecklers you sparred,
also with the Cops you haggled,
didn't Christ say it would be hard?

From the Bowery to Times Square, Columbus Circle,
thirty years I recall—serving Christ in N.Y.C.,
dad...you've seen it all!
What a reunion up in Glory, no doubt in my mind at all,
listening to Jesus, Abraham and Moses,
and the Jewish Apostle Paul.

Send him my regards; you named me after him,
tell my mother I love her, and I'm not feeling grim.
Regards to my sister Diana...Oh, there's so much
to say---but I'll save everything...for that Wonderful Day!

Again, thanks for accepting the Messiah Jesus,
He's my Lord and Savior too,
and though it was He Who saved me,
I won't mind saying thanks to you.

So I'll see you up there with all your friends
with the same Jesus you once shared,
in that wond'rous Land called Heaven...
which for you He had prepared.

Prov.22:6

Jesus is the Same

Jesus my friend is ever near,
twenty-four hours each day of the year.
He'll never desert nor disappear. . .
Jesus my friend is always there!
He will not change nor go away,
He doesn't dim like an earthly ray,
nor could His great love ever fray;
Nay, every minute of every day.
Jesus is faithful to His Name.
Time and Eternity hold no claim.
Aren't you glad that Jesus came?
Jesus, Jesus, ever the same.

Heb.13:8

God's Easter Gift

The Lord has risen. . .so let us sing!
Praise God. . .since death has lost its sting!
Lift up your voice, lift high your head--
He lives forever. . .Who once was dead!
They once nailed Jesus to a cross. . .
when Hell itself turned out full force!
For three days hence He took repose. . .
but on the third day—up He rose!
Through this the greatest triumph gave,
By conquering sin, Hell and the grave!
Let sceptics squeal. . .their rumors say. . .
There stands an empty tomb today!
Let Christians all their praise uplift,
Eternal Life's--God's Easter Gift!
1Cor.15:19-20

Make Sure To Do It Now!

The Gospel call goes out to all:
To the rich, the poor, the slow the bright.
But why do men refuse it so?
Because "they love darkness rather than light!"
Yet the most important Message ever...
which truly, the whole world needs to hear:
Is the 'Soul Saving Message of Jesus the Savior,
so that for Eternity---they might prepare!
Today, man's heart is not getting better,
'though his 'toys of technology' seem so great!
But two things man can never by-pass:
That is 'God's Judgment', and 'death's certain fate'!
You can play-act, fool many people,
even yourself with: "I'm good enough"!
But risk not your soul, Eternal and priceless,
by ignoring Jesus Christ or by 'calling His bluff'!
For Jesus now calls all souls to repentance, saying:
"Look unto Me, and be saved, perish doubt!"
For you never can know what might be on the morrow,
for the days are yet perilous, and time's running out!

So whatever mistakes you've made in this life,
whatever misgivings, successes or strife,
No matter your past, your hopes for the future,
make sure that your name's in
"The Lamb's Book of Life"!

2 Cor. 6:2

Whose Grace is Sufficient

Though we may be weak, still our Jesus is strong--
And when often weary—still He bears us along.
Praise the One Who's omniscient,
 and Whose Grace is sufficient,
 and His Spirit says..."Child, you belong"!
There's not ever a plight nor a problem that presses.
There's not ever a trouble nor a struggle that stresses.
 But always His Message to our hearts He addresses:
"Child, My Grace is sufficient for thee".

O what blessed assurance, Heaven's solace sublime,
Heaven's love, Glory's foretaste, with victory divine,
While in deepest despair, there is true peace of mind,
When His Grace is sufficient for thee.

Oh, whenever you think you're bereft of all wealth,
and maybe by chance, you've been--
left on the shelf. . .
and also the hour seems nearing 'the twelfth',
Christ Himself is sufficient for thee!

Since we're only sojourning,
our true home is not here,
Still His Eye's on the sparrow,
 in each trial in each trial He gives cheer.
And to know that in Glory someday He'll appear...
seems to make the Cross lighter we bear.

So take heart fellow Pilgrim...the future is bright,
'cause the Lord is returning, and He **never said... "might"**!
So with Paul, nigh "Pearled Portals" say:
 "I have fought a Good Fight,
and His Grace was Sufficient for me."

2 Cor. 12:9

If God Be for Us

If God would go before us,
we needn't dread the foe,
if we're led by His Spirit,
we need not fear earth's snare below?
We oughtn't e'er go backwards,
by Grace we shall not yield,
for we are more than conquerors,
through 'Faith's almighty shield'!

We wear Salvation's helmet,
though the Foe charge as a flood.
Our heart's breastplate is guarded. . .
Christ's Righteousness and Blood!
His peace, His Cross our Message,
our Gospel feet are shod,
"glad tidings", sound the Trumpet,
and Preach the Word of God!

Our weapon, the Sword of the Spirit,
none less we dare to take,
might evil principalities...
Hell's powers shall surely break!

Yet looking unto Jesus,
by grace we shall advance,
while conquering death's dominion,
'neath His Cross we take our stance!

Rom.8:31

If God be for us, who can be against us?

By Faith in Love

By faith, I'll put my trust in Jesus,

for by His Grace I shall succeed.

For He will prosper, heal, protect me—

while supplying ev'ry need.

'Cause if my mind is stayed on Jesus,

Hence, His perfect peace I'll find;

as His Word brings transformation—

strength and healing to my mind.

As I seek to praise and worship,

More His blessing I shall have.

And wait in stillness for His Spirit—

Freely flow like healing salve!

So priceless is His wond'rous Spirit,

None other Refuge need I go,

Where by His faith and loving Presence,

by grace my faith shall ever grow.

Gal. 5:6b

"Faith that worketh by love."

Thy Will Be Done

To trust Thy Grace to work Thy plan,

O Lord may I now understand,

 That might I trust Thy will for me,

as You direct my destiny.

 Not by self-will nor human might-

we walk by faith and not by sight.

That with Thy plan revealed in me,

by faith my future I might see.

So now, Lord Jesus, take my self-will;

my heart--that space. . .only You can fill.

Thus grant me grace to face each test,

 and thus embrace Thy way as best!

May all my hopes and dreams be Thine,

As with each care. . . I now resign.

Prov.3:6

Jesus, The Hope That I Have

I've got such a Hope, all earth's doubts shall not quell,
Since now that I'm Saved, with my soul it is well.
Who from being a sinner which was headed for Hell,
 Now through Christ I've a Hope of which words cannot tell!

This Hope which I've got, this poor World knows of naught,
This wonderful peace and release that I'd sought,
For so long while in sin, my heart had been caught,
'til unto the sweet "Mercy Seat" I was brought!

To the "Chiefest of Sinners," basest, vile, depraved,
yet by coming to Jesus, now stand Gloriously Saved!
Yes, thank God, Heaven's Highway by God's Grace has been paved.
Thank You Jesus, this Hope even transcends the grave!

Not through hemming and hawing in some vague wishfulness,
whereby day after day there's that 'quizzical guess'.
Still hoping and groping in some "educated mess"...
no, this Hope that I have is "affirmative yes"!

'Cause this Hope that I have is Christ living in me,
Who is able and wishes to do "equally",
If by faith you will kneel beneath Calvary's Tree,
Through Christ's Blood---Glory's Hope is A SURE GUARENTEE!

Col.1:27   Heb.6:19

Just a Carpenter

By the whispering waters of blue Galilee,
there appeared a mere carpenter that all Israel might see.
Although humble yet wise, still He had no degree,
Who without a beginning. . .hailed from all Eternity!
Without anything special that would give Him away,
just an unassuming rabbi, a mere Jew of His day.
From an unrenowned village, with some fishermen nearby,
Who came not to be famous, but to suffer and die!
Just His Spirit and demeanor which drew people to Him—
With His words strong but gracious—filled with love to the brim!
Often children came to Him. . .lepers, blind beggars too,
While the demons ran from Him,
Since His Person they knew!
From a mountain, or water-well, from a boat He would teach,
to the outcasts or to scholars,
God's Message He'd Preach!
Some believed Him, some would leave Him,
Yet His Words gave men hope,
That right down through the ages--have such infinite scope!
For the Words of this Man were not words that would fade,
For by the Words of this Carpenter--
Hence, were all the Worlds made!
Then let us draw near Him---Who is Heaven's only Door!
For none else, but this Carpenter offers Life Evermore!

Matt.15:33

Through Christ Alone

Just a sinner
Saved by Grace,
Thanks to Jesus,
Who took my place,
While once my sins
caused such disgrace,
But thanks to Him...
There's not even a trace!
I could never merit
Heaven's Prize,
Despite my many, endless tries!
My heart still harbored
fear and lies,
'til Jesus—
drew me to the Skies!
For not by noble deeds
We've done,
Nor to the mighty... the race is won,
Nor to the righteous... **no, not one,**
But simply trusting
God's own Son!
Might we inherit **Heaven's** Place,
And see our Savior, face to face.
So do not let this message waste!
Trust Christ, alone--
Be Saved by Grace!

Eph.2:8-9
"From shades of night, to plains of light, O praise His Name...He lifted me."

107

We Shall Walk with Him in White

We shall walk with Him in white
when we behold The Lamb so bright.
No more sunset, no more night,
when we shall walk with Him in white!
We shall cast our crowns before Him,
only bliss and never blight.
We shall crown Him King of kings,
what sight, to walk with Him in white.
But most of all to be with Jesus,
joy has never reached such height...
forever with the Lord in Heaven,
and be with Christ, and walk in white.

The King of kings, the Prince of Glory,
dear Rose of Sharon, my soul's delight.
 We shall see Him, and be like Him,
to walk and talk with Him in white.

Rev.3:4,5

If Christ Would Come Today

Is thy soul right with God,
if Christ would come today,
and were to stand before His Throne,
called from this house of clay?

Your name's in Heaven,
each sin's forgiven,
God's grace you did accept,
His robe of righteousness you wear,
Christ's covenant you've kept?

The Savior's thine, all's right with God,
your sins under the Blood,
already passed from death to Life,
no longer to be judged?

Do you know without a doubt,
and can you truly say,
that you would be with Him in Heaven,
if Christ would come today?

"Therefore, be ye also ready, for in such an hour
as ye think not. . .the Son of man cometh."
Matt. 24:44

I Give Christ the Credit

I give all the credit to Jesus,
my Savior and dear friend,
for all the perfect gifts,
which He to me did lend.
The privilege of bringing the lost
to the fold,
of singing the Gospel
that never grows old.
The honor of preaching the Word
of the Lord,
more powerful than a hammer,
a fire or a sword.
The privilege of standing for Christ
in His stead,
the wonder of raising those spiritually dead.
Oh, great responsibility. . .
 to no angel is given.
The credit goes to **Jesus,**
Who makes life worth living.

Gal.6:14

All that we think we possess or own is really only on loan
to us from God. . .that we might live for His Glory!

Wait on God

Don't step out without God's Power,
be sure to be endued,
'cause Satan as a roaring lion,
by him you will be chewed!
Don't launch out as in God's battle
fighting in the 'flesh',
be sure to have on 'God's full Armor'…
and 'Manna' that is fresh!
Do not depend on your own wisdom,
seek His, sent from the Throne.
Be sure to use "God's Mighty Weapons",
not those of your own.

Be led by Him,
trust in His Grace,
your mind and soul restored.
Stay in the Word, so walk in Jesus,
for the Battle is the Lord's.

2 Cor.10:4-5, Eph.6:13-17 Put on the whole Armor!

"It is good to wait quietly for the Salvation of the Lord." Lam.3:26

* Wait…Patiently-Psa.37:7, Quietly-Psa.62:1, Trustingly-Psa.37:7,
Expectingly-Psa.27:13, Steadfastly-Psa.27:14, and…
Standing on God's Word- Psa.130:5

Christ's Temptation

The Spirit drave Christ to the desert,
whence fasting forty days,
So fought the Devil on Adam's level:
Being tempted sundry ways.

"Pray, if Thou be the Son of God,
hence turn these stones to bread."
But Christ gave answer, "Nay, 'tis Written:
By God's Word shalt man be fed!"

Then brought Him up unto the Temple,
said, "Darest Thou leap down?
Shalt not be given His Angels' charge,
lest perish to the ground?"

Again spake Christ, "Knowest thou 'tis Written:
Ne'er shalt thou tempt the Lord?"
Still, subtle Satan, frustrated, waitin',
twice beaten...hemmed and hawed.

'Til last advanced...gave Christ to glance
vast earthly kingdom thrones.
"All this I'll deal, if Thou wouldst kneel,
and worship me alone."

Christ spake the Word saying: "Get thee hence!"
Thus fled the Devil smitten.
God's Word in might, put him to flight,
whilst Christ spake...'what was Written'!

Heb.4:12, 15

"And they overcame him by the Blood of the Lamb and by the Word of their
testimony." Rev,12:11

Long Spake Isaiah

(Sung to the melody of "Hatikvoh")
'Our Hope'-- the Isreali National Anthym.

A Light has dawned in Israel,
might Jacob see it glow—
the Law, the Psalms, the Prophets—
the Scriptures clearly show.
Weary were the 'Chosen Ones'
who waited, but in vain,
for when Jehovah's Son had come,
the Lamb of God was slain.

Shema Yisrael, "The Lord thy God is One,
and this Light is Yeshuah ... God's Only Son."
Long spake the Prophets: "A King to dwell
in Israel...making 'full atonement'...
Yeshua--Emmanuel."

For the Law no more availed...
Though they travailed, gave sacrifice.
For when the 'Age of Grace' took place,
Golgatha did suffice.
The stone was rolled, and up from 'Sheol', arose--
God's plan was done.
Then sent the 'Ruach Ha Kodesh',
through Whom in Him we're one!

Shema Yisrael, "The Lord thy God is One",
and this Light is Meshiach, God's only Son!
Long spake Isaiah: "El Gibor, Sar Shalom,
Ha dom kaporah...Yeshua, Emmanuel."

Isa.53:1

Return, O Israel

Return O Israel, ye sons of Jacob,

shake off thine unbelief.

For thy Messiah yet hast come,

To give thy soul relief.

My heart I gave with arms outstretched

as sweetest summer rain.

My love for you given to undo

Two centuries' grief and pain.

To thee especially, my first-born son,

The "Apple of my Eye";

My Holy prophets had been sent…

My Son, Who came to die!

Thou wouldst not see, thine eyes made blind,

As Moses wore a veil,

Be freed of sins and sorrows,

And freed of Jacob's wail!

But still you wandered—stiff neck blind--

Refusing to receive,

the Grace of God midst **miracles**,

and **chose not** to believe!

Your fathers longed and hope to see

This Promise so fulfilled,

Still when Messiah proved Himself--

Thy people stood self-willed.

O, Jerusalem, Jerusalem,

How I would have gathered thee--

As a hen gathers up her chicks

But you would not come to Me.

Thou hast no **dam Kappara** still,

For religion cannot atone.

And what might pay the **price for sin**...

But **blood**. . .and mine alone.

Matt. 23:37

(**Dam kappara** in Hebrew means **blood atonement**.)
Lev.17:11

Still I Will Follow Thee

I've ne'er deserved to serve Thee Lord,
Though follow Thee I will;
As when I think the sins You've borne,
When climbing Calvary's Hill.
I am not worthy, Lord to touch
The Cross where Thou didst die,
But if I may but linger near,
Or even follow by.
Ne'er might I earn to be Thy son,
But love Thee I shall do,
Though sauntering, sinful-self, undone,
By Grace, I shall pursue.
I am not worthy to approach
Thy Sacred—Matchless Throne,
But Thou hast opened Heaven's door,
And there shall be my Home.
O bid me take Thy Word so blest,
Or sing Thy Sweetest Name,
To tell some weary-wandering soul
The reason why You came.
Forgive me Lord for acting frail,
If murmuring I might do.
I've ne'er deserved to even serve,
Still, I will follow You.

Matt. 8:8

To Whom Much Is Forgiven

Once Jesus entered Simon's house
where Pharisees were at—
where soon came in a prostitute,
Who near to Jesus sat.
They glanced towards Jesus—
so self-righteous—
while tears fell by His feet.
One soon remarked: "Were He a prophet,
He would have changed His seat!"
Still lovingly, knelt by His side,
while softly fell each tear.
Then took some rarest, sweet perfume,
and wiped them with her hair.
She bathed Christ's feet with tears of love,
with broken heart was driven.
As then spoke Christ, while standing up:
"Daughter—thy sins be all forgiven!"

"For he who's been forgiven little,
like manner, loveth such.
But he did cherish and love much more
who was forgiven much."

Luke 7:47

117

God's Love Was Shown

God showed His Love at Christmas time,
Two thousand years ago,
While Angels spoke the Greatest News,
midst Shepherds bending low.
The Christ of God, the Prince of Peace--
So lay in meager style.
The Word made Flesh—the Heaven-sent News,
That man be reconciled!
God's love first shown unto His own,
Who would not Christ receive,
But cruelly mocked while sinners flocked,
God's loving heart was grieved.
Through Gospel Preaching, prayer.
Today God's love is shown again:
Yet hearts are cold, with sin are bold,
While many do not care.
Too busy buying cards with "Rudolph",
Yet won't accept a "tract"...
But sing of "Yuletide" and Santa's "Sleighride",
With haste. . .their gifts unpack!
Pray, might they see the Truth of Christmas,
Though given so long ago...
WHEN GOD SO LOVED THE WORLD, CHRIST CAME!
Their hearts the truth might know.

Rom.5:8
Love was when.....God became a man!

What Night Was This?

Who sleeps so sweet in manger low,
so humbly-wrapped 'neath Sacred Glow?
What poor estate an infant laid,
Yet Royalty, rare homage paid?
With lambs and oxen feeding by—
Yet Seraph—Chorus stream the sky!
What sign in time, at last fulfilled—
"A Jewish mother, Virgin still!"
What night of mere antiquity...
"That Changed the Course of History!"
For 'twas the Night, past reason's span,
Whence God Himself, became a man!

Isa.9:6

In the Mystery of Night

With guiding star midst night so chill,
with dreams might only God fulfill.
 In stillness of a night obscure,
Prophetic mysteries hailed of yore.
From Heaven's Throne,
 'neath Glory's shroud,
Creator's Word again endowed.
Of Blessed Hope and Life anew,
Of God with us and Heaven too!
So this He did, and did not tarry,
The Night that Christ was born of Mary.

Great is the Mystery of godliness...
God was Manifest in the flesh. 1 Tim.3:16

Not Many 'Wise' Receive God's Gift

Messiah, Jesus, Prince of Peace,
God's gift to all mankind,
for all the Grace and Truth of God,
in Jesus you shall find.

That was the Message told to Shepherds,
mid fields they watched their flock.
The Royal Decree thus sent by Angels,
of lowly humble stock.

Not to Herods, nor to Caesars,
'cause Truth they had not sought.
For so few mighty, 'wise or noble'
give heed to God's Report.

Though few 'wise people' still seek Jesus,
who cross that humble rift,
thus pass death's Judgment unto Life,
receive God's Christmas Gift!

1 Cor.1:26

Wise men **still** seek Him!

I Love the Lord Because

I love the Lord with all my heart,
for He's been good to me.
Just knowing Him for Who He is
brings true prosperity.
I'll worship Him for Who He is,
not 'cause of earthly things,
But peace and joy which comes because
I serve the King of kings.
I have been blessed just to possess
His truth my soul's embraced.
As I was drawn, my heart reborn,
by God's almighty grace.
So blessed am I to be His child,
such wealth one cannot buy;
not just down 'here', but over 'there',
midst mansions in the sky!
Yes, I'm adopted into God's family,
on His hands my name's engraved,
and praise and love Him for Who He is,
for by Him. . .I've been saved!

1Jn.4:10

The Son of God

God loved the word so much He sent Christ Jesus,
that whosoe'er believes Him shall not die,
but shall have Life, and have it everlasting!
For as Christ lives, even so, shall you and I.
"For this is Life, that they might know Jehovah,
And Jesus Christ", thus did my Savior pray.
And gave His life, thus tasting death for every man,
That was God's plan, the Cross,
there was no other way.

In Him was Life, that lighted men's hearts everywhere.
A Light Divine, death's darkness could not hide.
Abundant Grace and Truth, His words gave blessed hope.
The Son of God came to be crucified.

On Calvary's hill there crucified the Prince of Life.
No greater Love was shown at any time.
They nailed His hands, His feet, and pierced
His precious side.
God's judgment laid, sin's wages paid,
All for my crime.

So Christ Himself paid my sin's debt at Calvary;
Who made the Worlds, went to the Cross for me.
Such infinite Grace, no song nor poem can ever express...
Only myself, my heart, I give to Thee.

John 3:16

The Love of God

O love of God, from Heaven sent,
No mind can know its full extent.
Nor words of man could prose expound,
The love of God that knows no bound.

Ev'n every planet, flower or tree,
Tell just a sampled small degree.
Or awesome sunrise o'er loftiest peaks,
Nor calmest caverns, nor forest speaks.
Nor deepest depth of ocean swells,
As God in Christ's great love indwells.

How much of God's love can we see—
Would far surpass Eternity.
Still who could fathom such future stored,
For those in Christ who love the Lord!

What tongue can tell its full extent—
The love of God from Heaven sent.
But if God's love you'd chance to see…
Then take one glance at Calvary.

1 Jn.4:10

None Compared

There never was a dearer Person
In all the ranks of men,
That ever spread such sweet compassion,
Nor lived a truer Friend.
None ever loved nor kindly cared
Compared to which God gave,
As when Christ trod Golgotha's Hill,
From Hell, man's soul to save.
Where did appear a better Savior,
What greater ransom given,
Would e'er compare with Christ so dear,
Could bring our souls to Heaven?
There's no love like the Savior's love,
however far you look,
Nor greater Story as Christ's Great Love,
That's written in God's Book.

Matt.12:42

"He's the Lilly of the valley, the Bright and Morning Star...
He's the fairest of ten thousand to my soul."

HOW MIGHT IT BE?

How might it be...

That He'd become like you and me?

To condescend—become our Friend...

Forever change our destiny!

He saw our plight that fateful night...

And chose to go and live below...

Bearing our sins, our griefs and woe.

Still in a manger bed...in a starlit night,

His Father's will...a Cross in sight.

And chose to die upon a Tree,

become a man, like you and me!

Then bow our heads, with Praise uplift,

With thanks for God's 'Unspeakable Gift'!

What wond'rous love, how might it be...

When God became like you and me?

John 1:14

Job

There once lived a man whose name was Job
from an ancient town named Uz:
perfect and upright in all his ways,
if ever a person was.
His goods were plenteous, his substance great,
so seemed he had everything made.
His heart was pure and even more,
his faith could never be swayed.
Now along came the devil one ominous morn,
with his usual sedition and scorn.
But God said to Satan: "Hast thou e'er considered Job?
None as faithful nor grateful was e'er born".
But the devil then uttered,
having paced to and fro,
in scheming nefarious tones,
"That Job should but only ever fear God for naught?
Ah, afflict even one of his bones."
Then God said: "So go, hence to act as thou wilt,
but do thou no harm to his soul."
So Satan went forth, with his countenance wroth,
wreaking havoc and taking his toll!
Job's seed he'd destroyed, his cattle and wealth,
his poor body all covered with boils.
His own wife retorted: "Curse God now and die,
and so rest from all of thy toils."
"What meaneth this Lord---
while prostrate...bemoaned:
Was it my kin or my sin which I'd done?"
Then came three comforting counselors along,
spewing out 'Pearls of Wisdom' they'd spun.
But not even one could settle Job's trial,
and brought more confusion at best.
But just righteous Job, faithful and true
was determined that he pass the test!

But yet after he'd realized Who God really was,
and what a mere mortal was he,
Job thus bowed his head, wherefore he instead,
rent forth from his heart's inner plea:
"Though my life He should slay,
all I have take away,
for he taketh as well as He giveth.
Whence this flesh turn to dust,
still in God will I trust,
hence shall see my Redeemer…
Who Liveth!"

Job 19:25-26

If Only

I know my life would be alright,
If I just walk within the Light.
My fears and worries all would fade—
If I but only stopped and prayed.
I know all things would be O.K.,
If I just took the time to pray.
And called upon the "One Who Can",
Who holds each planet in His Hand.
And then my life would be so fine,
If with the Master I would dine.
Then shall my life be one of faith—
And live as "Hebrews-Eleven" saith.
O, keep my mind in perfect peace,
And cause my faith Lord to increase.

Isa.26:3

Keep the faith and the faith will keep you!
For we walk by faith and not by sight.

Jacob's Ladder

Jacob lay to sleep one night,
his pillow was a stone.
'Neath the star filled secret night,
slumbered there alone.
Thoughts of solace filled his mind
how God had promised him,
reassuring Isaac's blessing
to all of Abraham's kin.
So took his sleep in solace lay
as nothing else did matter;
'twas there as prayer envisioned it,
appeared a golden ladder!
Ascending up and reaching to
the foot of Heaven's door;
so awesome was blest Jacob's dream
he'd never seen before.
As on each rung an angel stood
descending where he slept,
and on the very top of it
the God of Heaven stepped.
And spoke confirming words of comfort
with God's own command,
to multiply the seed of Jacob,
possessing Jordan's Land.

Jesus, He is Jacob's Ladder,
coming down to earth,
giving us His greater promise
through God's Second Birth.
Even as you ascend, my friend,
your soul shall be made gladder.
Thus receive the Lord by faith,
by climbing Jacob's Ladder.

Gen.28:11-13

Like Unto Moses

Moses, servant used of God...
though raised in Pharaoh's Court,
was steadfast, loyal to his God,
his heart could not be bought.
And chose to suffer for a season
with the lot of those--
whom God selected for a reason,
thus God's will he chose!

As Israel bowed 'neath bitter bondage,
all that they could bear,
hence did they pray, day after day,
'til God had met their prayer.
God's time drew nigh that Moses lead
the seed of Abraham.
"Lest they request whose name
whence came, "Proclaim--I Am that I Am!"
Hence last convinced, went forth to Pharaoh,
ten times had Moses pled.
Not 'til the end did Pharaoh bend,
whence found his first-born dead.
Then passed the ghastly grim 'Death-Angel'
o'r the house The Blood was stayed.
Thus showed the merciful Grace of God
towards them His Word obeyed.

Delivered Israel out of Egypt,
great Miracles they saw:
the Red Sea parted,
God's Plan was charted,
when Moses gave the Law.

Though Moses rose as Great Deliverer,
and Giver of the Law,

which pointed as a 'Path to Christ',
Who is the actual Door.

Yeshua, He's our great Deliverer,
God sent His Pascal Lamb.
Embodied Truth and Life Eternal,
Himself, the Great I Am.

Heb.11:24-25

The Law was given by Moses but Grace and Truth came through Jesus Christ.
John 1:17
No man can keep the whole, Law but Jesus kept it all for us wherefore by faith we
have been given His imputed Righeousness. Thanks be to God!
"Therefore being justified by faith we have peace with God through our Lord Jesus
Christ." Rom.5:1

He That Hath the Son

Many may claim---that they have God,
while Jesus they reject!
But if we hear what Christ had said,
their "thinking's incorrect"!

Who hath not Whom the Father sent...
the Father knoweth not!
Whence their false "Concept" of "their God",
is merely all they've got!

But he who hath the Blessed Christ,
God's only begotten Son,
hath both the Spirit and the Father,
for all these Three are One!

1 Jn.2:23

God's Word says it, I believe it, and that settles it!

Brave Daniel Took His Stand

The Prophet Daniel, man of God,

With faith as strong as iron--

No force from Hell his faith could quell,

Not fire, beast nor Lion!

No king's command by Satan's plan

to threaten nor to slay him,

No doubt nor fear could halt his prayer

to intimidate or sway him!

He vowed ne'er bow to golden idols

by any pagan nation,

Defying odds 'gainst heathen gods...

What perilous situation!

But prayed to God three times each day—

faced towards Jerusalem.

Thus framed, conspired by Satan's hired--

evil, treacherous men.

Through many tries, with wicked lies...

sent him to a lion's den.

Still never did he compromise,

on God he would depend.

Then finally thought-- they'd had him caught...at last his doom was sure!

But an Angel sent from God came down—

and shut the lion's jaw!

(cont'd)

Ol' Nebuchanezzar, Babylon's king-

'the greatest ever to reign',

thus bragged of all his mighty works—

(made dwell with beasts insane!)

Beltshazzar's dream once troubled him,

told: "Soon his reign would fall...

Found wanting, weighed in the balances"—

'hand-written on the wall'!

Nebuchanezzar, Beltshazzar, Darius, Cyrus,

Great kings who ruled the land...

However, lest God had granted power—

No monarch's word would stand!

It was Daniel's gift of prophesy

to interpret each king's dream,

would naught but prove that Daniel's God

would one Day reign Supreme!

Still faithful Daniel stood each test,

though in a pagan land,

still trusted God---though times grew hard,

Brave Daniel took his stand!

Absolom, My Son. . . O My Son

There once lived a ruler in Israel long ago:

A shepherd, a Psalmist, a king—

Who knew what it meant to follow the Lord,

Who did write, play his harp, fight and sing!

He was chosen by God to rule over His people,

As they followed his 'God's purposed" lead.

In the Psalms called "a man after God's own heart",

 As he led with "Anointing" indeed.

Now he had a son who in envy conspired,

Who had planned to take over his throne!

Same as Satan once tried to take over Heaven,

Til at last to the earth he was thrown!

So he gathered up men to usurp the king then,

Whom he drew with his wit and his charm;

 being stately and fair, with his proud 'head of hair'. . .

Til the king heard the news in alarm!

Now the battle turned bad for the king's rebel lad,

And thus went the fate of his son.

Through the woods he was chased

as he tried to escape,   (cont'd)

so he fled the king's men and did run!

With swift steed he did flee,

'til was snagged by a tree and so helplessly

hanged in mid-air!

Whence the king's men pursued

and so ended the feud

who then smote him....

As he hung by his hair!

Soon this sad news was brought

To this king so distraught—

Who in tears sorely asked:

"What was done?"

Hence the wails of a king

Throughout Israel did ring:

Crying: Absolom. . .my son, Absolom

 my son!

2 Sam.18:33

 The Bible says: "Pride goeth before destruction,

and a haughty spirit before a fall." Prov.16:18

A Missionary's Farewell

I've needs to go,
I shall not stay.
To God I must account some day.
His will, my aim,
and vow ne'er turn
from following Christ—
the plow not spurn.
But follow Him where'er He'll lead,
and trust His grace for every need.
That I might say
when ends life's mission:
"I had obeyed
The Heavenly Vision".
  Acts 26:19

Jesus said: "Go ye into all the world and preach the Gospel and lo I am with you always, even unto the ends of the Earth." Mark 16:15. Always Good News!!

Raindrops

Raindrops falling from the sky—

Silver beads from Heaven.

 Kiss the Earth to tender it.

Fill its fruit with sweetness.

Cover ev'ry branch and bough,

Breakforth with its joyous jewels,

 Sparkling over grass and ground...

Silver beads from Heaven.

 Zech.10:1 (a)

Did Jonah Ever Have a Diploma?

Did Jonah ever receive a 'Diploma'?
Where did he graduate?
Some say: "Fish University"—
while served time as 'de-bate'!
God said: "Go up to Nineveh."
Jonah said: "Next stop, Tarshish."
But God now turned his tour around,
prepared a 'Great Big Fish'!
How that ship shook, the waves now growled,
as darkness filled the deep.
Each sailor cried out to his god...
lay Jonah...fast asleep.
'The lot fell on Jonah'...they questioned him,
said how he'd fled the Lord.
With ship off course, to spare much loss...
they tossed him overboard!
A timely fish which God prepared,
Poor prophet was no winner.
By Sovereign swoop---'fast order scoop',
poor Jonah served...as dinner.
Three days and nights, held such a 'vigil',
(his own soul, not Revival).
Then soon enough, he was coughed up...
and sailed him like a tidal.
Now 'wise' but wet, with some regret,
What 'Transcript' did he need?
And what 'diploma' presented Jonah...
his 'sermon-notes'...'Sea-weed'.
"Forty days, and Nineveh shall be destroyed!"
the "Preaching bid by God".
The King nor his Officialdom
never checked his Clergy card.
To which "deep School" did Jonah go?
The answer's rather clear:
He went to "Fish University",
with "Three long nights in Prayer".

(You cannot run from the Spirit of God.)

And Would See Christ

Above all things I might desire—
I would seek Thy will, Thy way inquire.
Despite all things this life may grant,
Yet still my thirsting would pant—
Unto Thy courts my soul would flee...
to drink Thy Word...and taste of Thee.
If just one thing...my heart's desire,
To follow the path of my Messiah—
Of all life's goals...there's nothing higher!

And would see Christ!
This most I crave,
Whose Palace left to spoil the grave.
No greater beauty could I see,
Than He who came and died for me.
And evermore this joy possess—
I would see Christ,
And nothing less.

Jn.12:21

For now we see through a glass darkly;
 but then face to face. 1 Cor.13:12

About Psalm One

Receive your counsel from God's Word
and thus you shall be blest;
thus choosing not the godless way,
though often be 'hard pressed'.
Though everyone around should guess,
"Perhaps you're not all there?"
Still turn from them unto thy God,
and cast on Him your care.
Dwell on His precepts day and night,
arise a fruitful plant.
And so through Jesus, richly thrive,
and cast away each 'can't'.
Let the streams of Living Waters
freshen soul and spirit...
open to the Shepherd's voice
so when He speaks, you'll hear it.
The wicked's way shall surely cease
and never find true peace.
The righteous man shall surely stand,
and prosperously increase.
So walk in Christ, the Way, the Truth,
His Counsel freely get,
that when in Glory you'll arrive,
His Truth you'll not regret.

Psa. 1: 1

You'll never go wrong when you follow
the Good Shepherd... Jesus!

What I Truly Love the Most

I love Your crimson sunset sky,
what portrait might compare?
With colors bright, You gave man sight,
for music, made the ear.

The way You feed that lonely lark,
that lilts its little song.
The buttercup the sun wakes up,
to cheer the birds along.

The way You listen to my prayer,
as down upon my knees—
You watch me as You do each bird,
that sails on lofty breeze.

I love the way You save and keep,
Thy wondrous Plan of Grace.
And love the way You help me with
another day to face.

Oh, how I love these things you've done,
the ways You've made to please us.
But truly what I love the most...
is that You gave us Jesus!

Psa. 26:7

'Thanks be unto God for His 'Indescribable Gift' 2Cor.9:15

Lay It Aside

What is it beloved Christian friend,
that hinders you to run The Race?
Lay aside that weight which hinders you
from pressing into that Spirit led pace.

There's such a Cloud of Witnesses,
which urge us to that Vision and Goal.
Redeem the time the hour's late—
and what of many a Christless soul?
So don't turn back once you have started,
the laborers few, the Harvest great.
The times so perilous, Christ returning,
can't you see the Hour is Late?

Fight the Good Fight and ne'er retire,
Christ has pioneered the path.
Look to Him, the Lamb of Calvary,
For soon will come God's Day of Wrath.

What hinders you to trust His Promise,
Christ who is our Hope and guide,
has called us now to run with patience,
and said He'd never leave our side.

Heb. 12:2

Thank You

Thank You for this lovely day,
for shedding 'sunlight' on the way!
Now help me Lord to watch and pray,
That I might thus Thy Word obey.

Grant me grace for every need—
with faith to follow as You lead.
Peace to comfort my faint heart,
with faith to realize Who Thou art.

For standing by me in the way,
The gift to see another day!
For food and shelter, clothing too—
friends that ever might stay true.

Little things...like friendly smiles—
lending strength to go through trials.
For Jesus Christ and life anew...
for this life now...and Heaven too.

These thanks I give for blessing me,
but most of all. . .for Calvary.

Psa. 68:19

Little is much when God is in it.

Every breath is a gift from God!

I Know I'm Not Black

I know I'm not Black—I'm White—
But that's alright—what can I say?
Hey! God made me that way!
Colors are nice—but don't matter to me,
You see I'm free.
Though I live in this tainted nation—
I'm part of God's great creation.
I know history has its shame—
But it's where I'm going,
More than from where I came.
Is life fair? Ask Job, He'd been there.
But my real home's not here!

I don't need a name—a flag—or pride—
I know who I am inside.
I have love. It's all by Grace—not race,
Or human cause—let seekers pause—
And know that the soul is not of skin,
But from within—it's **God, or sin!**

Let me be scorned or more reviled,
But with my God—I'm reconciled.
Thank God, it is in Christ I stand,
hence free to love my fellowman.

Acts 17:26

It's not the skin problem, it's the sin problem.
For God so loved the World...His creation---
the entire human race! "Christ is for everyone"!

142

God's Love Made Real

The love of God Christ showed to sinners—
where does one begin?
Who left His Crown, His life laid down
laid waste the power of sin.

Such love of God, what joy from Heaven,
knowing we're His children.
What blessedness to hear His Words,
what honor to fulfill them.

Compared to earthly pride of life,
the World, the fleshly lust,
as in conclusion, this illusion,
would fall to thieves and rust.

Love cannot last when hearts are set
on things the flesh desires,
which differs largely from the things
of which God's Heart requires.

By trusting God through Jesus Christ,
through faith we're now made righteous,
and as we joy to do His will,
His fellowship delights us.

So let Christ's love be lived through us,
that whosoever sees us,
might truly see the love of God
made real through us in Jesus.

Jn.13:35

"This little light of mine...I'm gonna let it shine."

Speak of Jesus

I love to Speak of Jesus--
What joy to bring His Word!
Especially would I share it,
With those who've never heard.

With grace and deep compassion,
Unveil the Gospel call,
Hold forth the Savior's Message,
And not let one Word fall.

So would I point to Calvary,
To glimpse His love so vast,
And say how He hath pardoned,
My sins which now are past.

I love to bring Christ's message,
His words so true and dear,
And go forth, I shall tell it,
To people everywhere.

Rom. 1:16

"Tell me the story of Jesus, write on my heart
ev'ry word."   Old hymn

Prayer for Guidance

Jesus take my hand and guide me.
Lead me through each toilsome day.
Be my shield and staff beside me.
Shine Thy light upon the way.
Take my hand and lead me onward,
forward as my life goes on.
Strengthen me, my faith with kindness,
even after all is gone.
Mold my spirit in Thy sight, Lord,
even as the trials break through,
and the pathway seems so narrow…
more may I be drawn to You.
Teach me how to praise and seek Thee,
so might I grow pure and strong.
Be my joy and my Salvation,
through each day,
my whole life long.

Psa. 32:8

"Savior like a shepherd lead us;
much we need Thy tender care."
(Old Hymn Ira Sankey.)

Then That's the Time to Pray

When the heart feels down...and the spirit seems cold,
then that's the time to take hold... and be bold.
When the cares suppress, and life's trials abound,
and it seems as though God cannot be found.
When the heart seems cold and the hours pass,
and the Heavens seem they're made of brass.
And temptations come and the world annoys
with surmounting ills,
and there are no joys.
As life's dark clouds cast their gray dismay,
Beloved, more than ever, that's the time to pray!

Psa. 43:5

Help Me to Pray

Help me to pray Lord,
speak to my heart.
Lend my soul Thy Mind,
to know Who Thou art.
Though I'd stumble with great thoughts,
lift my heart to Thy Word.
Might I look just through Thine eyes,
only Thy voice be heard.
I ask nothing of "earth's toys",
but the joys of Thy Way.
I would love Thee and serve Thee. . .
now Lord, teach me to pray.

Luke 11:1

Three greatest gifts; Salvation the Bible and Prayer.

Whose Heart and Will's in God

I wish to find Thy path, dear God
and choose naught but Thy Will.
So grant me grace to find that place,
to know Thee and be still.
In truth I wish to seek Thy way,
Blest Shepherd of Thy fold,
and would not once be satisfied—
having all earth's wealth untold.
Did not I list in earnestness...
yet still had missed Thy call?
But Thy Word says, "A righteous man--
gets up, though times he'd fall."

You know my name...same as my frame,
each thought before Thy sight.
And this I'm sure, with heart that's pure,
You said You'd make things right.
You went to Calvary, took my place,
And there for me did die.
Then went right back to Heaven itself,
to prepare a Mansion on High.

My heart's content to know what's meant:
"With Thee, nothing's too hard",
and to know---"All things work together for good
to those who trust in God".

Psa.37:24

Trust Him where you can't trace Him.

Undeserving as I

He was despised and crucified,
that He might save man's soul.
Who made all things—seen and unseen;
Whom angels did extol.
Yea, Christ, God's dearest Lamb for me,
That Precious Blood was shed,
for such a one deserving not
to gaze upon that Head.
Oh, Sacred God and Holy Son,
from out the Father came,
Who offered up His soul for mine,
No merit might I claim.
Nothing to do--nor say could pay,
nor just one sin remove;
for one undone could ne'er deserve
Such love as He did prove.
Oh Christ, accept me as I am,
my plight I now confess.
So, might I plead Thy crimson flow,
and 'neath Thy Cross find rest.

1 Pet.3:18

We are saved by God's mercy, not by our merit;
by Christ's dying, not by our doing.

148

Grace to the Rescue

I once had struggled,
About to drown,
Without a life-raft,
Going down.
Chains of sin's gloom
Drawing back...
Life's fretful waves
Upon me stacked.
Darkness 'round me
Everywhere.
Bound by only night's despair.
No way out—no way free,
Only darkness did I see.
Just then I caught
A glimmering ray,
And heard a sweet voice:
"Look this way!"
I looked up...seeing Jesus,
It was He!
How lovingly He gazed at me.
Then stilled the storms,
And calmed life's sea,
dispelled my fears and set me free!
Tenderly, sweetly, what delight,
He chased away all pain and fright.
O, how I love Him,
How great is He,
Who by His grace,
had lifted me.

Titus 3:5

"Amazing Grace, how sweet the sound."

He Lives

The Lord has risen—what wondrous thought!
The battle's won, the victory's wrought.
So may we boast, as yet we sing—
deriding death...where is thy sting?

And bear the "Good News" to all men,
With surety—He lives again!
Be done away with mortal fears,
To offer hope to all who hears.

Let all in Him receive the prize,
For Christ Who suffered did arise!
And now has opened Heaven's Gates,
Eternal Life to all awaits.

At God's right Hand He now is seated,
The "powers of death" have been defeated!
For Christ has risen, His Word made good,
Come now believe, if so ye would.

Let ev'ry voice now boldly sing—
"O death, O death...where is thy sting?"
'Tis not just history which we read,
For Christ is risen, and lives indeed!

Luke 24:6

The death of Christ is a mystery...
The Resurrection of Christ is History!

Thy Touch

A touch of Thee from Calvary,
Push back the clouds of sin.
One touch from Thy dear nail-scarred Hand,
lets Heaven's Light come in.

O touch me now that I might know
no greater touch than this.
For with one gentle touch from Thee,
I'd know no greater bliss.

A touch of Thee from Calvary,
would turn the night to day.
A touch from Thy dear healing hand,
is all I ask and pray.

I ask not for the cares of life,
nor would I seek for much.
But one thing would I ask of Thee,
that I might feel Thy touch.

Mark 1:41

She touched the hem of His garment and instantly was made whole!
Then Jesus said to her: "**Be of good comfort. . .thy faith hath made thee
whole!**"

(A touch from Heaven can work wonders!)

A Prayer of Despair

Please dear God, I wish You'd heal,
or at least reveal as why I feel
this way right now so I can know,
at least the route that I must go.
I am upset, trials abound…
no one to help, no one around.
If it's not You, then all is grim…
O, please don't let the lights stay dim.
Please come quickly to my aid…
life goes on like a parade.
But here I'm empty, cold and lone,
like a disconnected phone.
Like a shattered heart that cries,
to ever strive but find no prize,
to find no light nor peace within,
but ever fallen amidst the din.
How I'd wish to do again,
and be encouraged once more to win.
But now I feel the door is shut…
please let me rise from out this rut!
Help me Lord to know there's hope.
I want to live, not merely cope.
Oh, give me hope, let me return—
might it just be "a lesson learned".
Don't leave me broken in grim despair.
The Bible says You truly care.
Please take away this present wound,
in Your Providence there's no ruin.
Please, dear God, cast me not down.
but cause Thy mercy to abound.
Heal Thy servant, heal Thy son,
complete Thy work which You've begun!

Psa.42:11

Be Encouraged

When you're down and feeling blue,

with the pain you're going through,

know that God knows what to do,

and His Word is always true!

When you seem to lack the zest,

sometimes feel 'you aren't blest',

Just be sure that it's a test,

and be sure that God knows best!

Ev'n when everything seems wrong,

Don't stop trusting, just stay strong,

While the Spirit brings a song,

Hidden strength will come along!

So don't doubt nor be upset,

'Cause His Grace and Peace you'll get,

Choose to trust and not to fret,

For Christ will not fail you yet!

Prov. 3: 5,6

In Everything Give Thanks

In everything give thanks to God,
This is His will for you.
Regardless of whatever trial
or thing you're going through.
In everything give thanks from Whom
Wise Sovereign mercies flow.
For 'tis the path of victory,
The way in Christ we grow.

Now thank Him for the sunshine new,
As well as at the dawn.
And thank Him in the darkness too...
When earthly dreams are gone.
Still serve Him with each breath He gives,
'Till we'll rise to "Jordan's Banks",
That come what may...midst night or day,
In everything....give thanks.

1Thess.5:18

When we 'thank,' we 'think' of all the wonderful things God has done for us on a
daily and 'Eternal basis'.
 Let it not be merely a traditional 'Thanksgiving Day' exercise in November as it is
for many, but a daily dedication with praise to Him.... from Whom all Blessings
flow!

Give Me a Song in the Night

Give me a song in the night, loving Lord,
send me a melody deep...
so all my soul, my heart and my mind,
can recount how You lovingly keep.
Give me a song when the hours grow long,
and much of life seems to go wrong;
when its shadows befall—
and my faith seems so small,
In the night, Jesus, give me a song.

Though my dreams would seem crushed,
mirth and music lie hushed,
and the worst might seem to impend;
send me a song in the night, dearest Lord,
whose worship and praise has no end.
Send me a sound of sunshine so sweet,
while life's last winter's sun has gone down.
Therein might I sing, giving thanks in all things,
whether to want or abound.

Give me a song in the night, loving Lord,
which life's storms with its clouds cannot blight.
That I might not just sing 'when the lark's on the wing',
Savior, send me a song in the night.

Job 35:10

Might We Learn This of Thee

We were made in God's image—for His Glory,
So to learn and obey His command;
And to fear Him, do justice, love mercy.
'Tis the duty of each man!
That we love, worship, trust, obey Him,
As we offer Him honor and praise,
then to love one another as He loved us--
then to follow and walk in His ways!
Whether Sunshine or tempest befall us--
Whether life brings us joy or bitter pain;
For the Bible says Godliness with contentment,
Shall always bestow us the greater gain!
For we brought naught to this world--on arrival,
Therefore, in like manner we shall leave,
And so, what have we got since we came here,
that we haven't from the Father so received?
While the vain things of this life seem to vex us,
And with problems we oft tend to fuss,
be compared to the Glory awaiting,
which the Savior has promised to us?
So to God be the Praise and the Glory,
As we give Him our honor and praise—
Therefore, help us, dear Lord to consider--
And to number and value our days.

Psa.90:12

So that we might apply our hearts to wisdom.

Choice

This temple in which we dwell...
is but a 'temporary shell'.
But the eternal 'inner person'
reports to Heaven...or else to Hell!
To reject the Savior Jesus,
and not believe His Name,
doth incur the wrath of God,
as with Hell's Eternal flame!

Christ proved—there's more beyond the grave!
Man's thoughts at best...a fraud!
For the Christian...to be absent from the body means--
to be present with the Lord!
For with Christ—'tis 'glorious bliss'...
and Hell's too horrible to explain!
The latter we best avoid,
and the former we can gain!

So, repent—get right with God--
receive God's free gift of Salvation!
To thus avoid the Lake of fire,--
Hell's Eternal Condemnation!

John 3:36

There's a Heaven to gain and a Hell to shun!

And Great Shall Be Thy Praise

How great Thou art, most holy God,
of mercy, endless grace,
Of infinite love, omnipotence,
Thy kindness doth embrace.

Thy wondrous, bounteous starry skies
above each snow--capped mount.
Yet greater wonder is man's soul,
as the stars—no man can count!

How dear the sunrise, fair the rose,
and vast the ocean tide.
Yet greater mystery, wondrous love,
when Christ on Calvary died.

Great God of grace, beyond man's thoughts,
Thy holy love transcends,
Indwelt in Christ upon the Cross,
Thy love that never ends.

How great Thou art—Thy loving heart,
as from Thy tomb whence raised.
Such great Salvation from Thy Great Son,
and great shall be Thy praise!

Psa.145:3 Psa.104:1

A Prayer for America

Now pray we that our country be
A Nation Wise and True,
Might righteousness, and holiness
Be kept in highest view.

And pray America would see
Her duty to release,
Her love for truth midst godliness—
Where man through Christ finds peace.

Might she revere her Savior's Name,
Wherewith doth guide her fate,
For when she ceases to be good,
She ceases to be great.

Then may she seek her highest goals.
Be free to do God's Will.
And when her foes amidst her rise,
her might, their voices still.

O pray, America wouldst stand,
With nobleness be shod—
Beneath her feet,
The Mercy Seat,
Find favor with her God.

1 Tim.2:1,2

When America ceases to be good...
she ceases to be great!

"God Bless America. . .Land that I love!"

In Honor I Shall Stand

What noble sight of great delight-
to see my flag yet wave!
And think of all the valiancy
whose hero's lives they gave!
 Midst families, fortunes, highest dreams,
because they loved this Land--
its mountains, plains and river-lanes;
they nobly took their stand!
 Their only goal was liberty,
 and all that freedom yields,
 o'er fields and plains,
 thru loss or gains,
 their pledge to God was sealed.
 Thru battles, storms and raging foes,
their fight was noble—true!
And with the victory which God did give--
was given for me and you!
 O flag so noble, of lovely sight,
of justice, truth so grand
that when I see thee passing by,
in honor I shall stand!

Prov.14:34

U.S. Army Vet '71-'72

One Nation, under God with liberty and justice for all.
"Long may our great flag wave!   "

160

I Am An American

I am an American—
A privileged, honored, thankful soul.
I am an American—
And thrilled to see my Country's flag unfold.
My land, my dreams, my pledge—in file I stood
and spent my time in Service—
for my Country's good.
But what of those who made such sacrifice—
to make this World a better place,
with blood paid such a price?

I see its woods, its mountains' streams,
Such blessings which God bestowed.
And know there's no better place on earth,
and think what I had owed.

I am an American—
Still hold its marvelous dreams:
Its schools, its Churches, its courts,
Its laws...each city brightly gleams.

It towers every nation.
Its beckoning Statue calls,
to give their tired and their poor,
without dividing walls.

Thus are we blessed of God—
because we hold His Name on High,
And that is why I love this Land
whose dreams shall never die...
I am an American.

Psa.33:12

Let Down Your Net

Came Jesus strolling by the Sea
of Lake Genneseret,
where seeing Simon, James and John,
who casting out their net—
heard Jesus speak the sweetest words,
the common people heard.
And as they sat there listening,
great miracles occurred!
When finished preaching, turned He to Simon
saying: "Launch out to the deep!"
But Simon answered, "Nay, but Master,
we've toiled with sundry sweep".
But did not falter to obey,
set forth within a wink,
enclosed such multitude of fish,
the boat began to sink.
Fell Simon then upon his knees,
cried, "I am a sinful man!"
But Jesus dearly loved him so,
and did not reprimand...
but beckoned Simon follow Him,
which choice he'd ne'er regret.
Hence, Simon's name was changed to Peter,
who put away his net
Hear Jesus calling now today,
as He did way back then,
to "let our nets down for a draught",
and go, and fish for men.
Who will go and follow Jesus,
launch out the Gospel net,
As Peter, James and John had done,
at Lake Gennesaret?

Luke 5:10-11

Holy Spirit

O gentle Spirit, sweet, endearing,
sent from God's own Holy Throne,
when You come to me and fill me,
I am never left alone.

Power of God and God the Power,
Comforter, Teacher, Helper, Guide,
illuminating, glorifying--
Christ alone, the Crucified.

Showing me Thy truth in Scripture,
convicting, soothing, cleansing fire,
Aiding me, protecting, loving,
reviving me when times I tire.

Holy Spirit, now hover o'er me,
anoint my heart, my hands, my feet,
until I reach the Gates of Glory,
make Thy workmanship complete.

Jn.15:26

The Holy Spirit is our comforter, guide, teacher, protector, defender,
Seal of our Redemption and Revealer of the Divine Person of Jesus Christ!

Lord, Help Me Write A Poem

Lord, help me write a poem that
some longing soul might know,
the Blessed Gospel of Thy Grace...
with love, let each word flow.
So might it bear the Greatest News
that ever has been told,
to hail the Message of God's Love,
endearingly, yet bold.
Let it spring forth a fragrance that
is neither harsh nor bland,
but just a simple telling truth
some soul might understand.
So would it reach some saddened heart,
with gladdening touch employ,
to cast away earth's doubtful ray,
then fill with Heaven's joy.
To tell how Jesus on that cross
Our sins and sorrows bore--
That in each line, its rhyme might chime—
The Good News evermore!
So may it be, when all is done,
beyond the poem I pen,
that Jesus Christ being lifted up,
might draw to Him all men.

John 12:32

Keep Your Eyes On Jesus

Keep your eyes upon the Savior.
for there's no better place to look.
Fix your eyes upon the Master--
find Him in that "Sacred Book".

And keep your eyes off from the "World's View",
its pomp, its glare. . .a mere facade!
But place your eyes upon Christ Jesus...
so spend some time alone with God.

And be not lured by things enticing....
Fleshly things that "war the soul".
Set your mind and heart on Jesus,
Let His example be your goal.

When darkness lurks and would engulf you,
and Satan's hosts would get you down,
still He is there in prayer to guide you,
bringing you to higher ground.

Still keep your eyes upon the Savior,
God's loving promise shall not fail.
Just keep on looking unto Jesus,
His loving grace shall yet prevail.

Heb. 12:2

None Else Like Jesus

I'm so glad that Jesus saved me.
With my soul I know 'tis well.
For since now my reach is Heaven,
   Never have I fear of Hell!

Now since Jesus is my Savior,
And I've given my heart to Him--
With His Precious Blood that saved me,
   Cleansed my heart and life of sin!

For He came to earth from Heaven,
   Did what no one else could do.
While He offers full Salvation,
and a life 'completely new'!

He has mercy, grace and pardon,
Peace and joy--all without price.
Ne'er there ever be another—
like my Savior, Jesus Christ!

John 6:68

When I found Jesus, I no longer needed to search for 'The Truth'!

The answer to 'life's quest' I'd searched for. . .I've found in Him alone!

About the author and the book

Written over a span of forty years, this collection of poetry, consists of various, sometimes challenging Bible topics for all ages, faiths, ideologies and backgrounds. These poems are neither modern nor abstract, but simple and direct, maybe sermon-like... exploring topics meaningful to the poet's heart.

In this collection of 170 Poems, Mr.Revenson's writings might be somewhat influenced by his living in New York City, his relationship with Christ--faith, hope, aspirations and even grief... but mostly joy! Each poem is followed by a relevant Scripture verse to give further enlightenment to help bring one closer to the Lord--the Source and purpose of each inspired poem!

In each poem, the writer seeks to glorify God, enlighten, encourage, entertain, and evangelize. Whether you are facing a challenge, renewing your faith or simply thanking the Lord for all His blessings, you may find something here which may fill your heart and edify your soul.

Paul Revenson was a N.Y.C. High School Spanish and E.S.L. teacher for twelve years, now a retired Home Care, Human Resource caseworker for New York City.

Paul enjoys playing the piano, singing hymns with inspiring words and writing as a means of sharing his faith with whosoever will hear him, even on the streets and subways of N.Y.C..

He is also of Jewish background.

www.ingramcontent.com/pod-product-compliance
Lightning Source LLC
Chambersburg PA
CBHW030258130626
46549CB00002B/582